S0-BDN-975

"A TRUE STORY THAT WILL MAKE YOU LAUGH, CRY AND BE GLAD YOU'RE ALIVE!"
—*Literary Guild Magazine*

Sheila Hocken lay in a hospital ward, waiting for the bandages to be removed from her eyes . . . waiting to learn if a surgeon's skill had worked a miracle.

It seemed too much to hope for. For already Sheila had known so very many miracles.

The miracle of parents who refused to let her feel apart. The miracle of Don, who loved her. And above all, the very special miracle of a dog named Emma . . .

EMMA AND I

Big Bestsellers from SIGNET

Emma and I

by
Sheila Hocken

A SIGNET BOOK
NEW AMERICAN LIBRARY
TIMES MIRROR

This book is dedicated to
John E. Coates

Some names of people and places have been changed, and certain
painful events in my life have not been mentioned since they are
not central to this book.

Acknowledgment

I wish to thank Lieutenant-Commander Jack Waterman, RD, RNR, without whose kind advice and help this book would not have been possible.

S.H.

Contents

Emma and I

1

A CHILD APART

When I was four years old, I managed to find my way down the garden path of my house to the front gate. Putting out a hand, I traced my fingers down the wrought iron until I felt the latch. Then I opened the gate, went out on the sidewalk and stood in my velvet dress listening. Listening for other children. Listening because that was the only way I could tell if they were out there playing.

From the other side of the road I heard the voices of little boys and the sound of something else—a ball bouncing against a wall or wooden gate. I called out, "Hello! Can I play with you? Can I come and play?"

The ball stopped bouncing and there was silence. Then one of the boys answered, "No, you can't. You couldn't play if you tried. *Cross-Eyes!*"

As I turned and felt my way back to the house, I heard the ball start bouncing again. I was puzzled, but not hurt, because I had no idea what the boys had meant.

"Mom! Mom, what does 'Cross-Eyes' mean? Why do the boys always call me that? Why won't they let me play with them?"

My mother's answer was always the same: "Sheila, they're bad boys. I've told you before, you mustn't try and play with them. They're very naughty."

"But why do they call me 'Cross-Eyes'?"

"They don't know any better. It's a very naughty,

1

rude name." Then she changed the subject, and brought out my teddy bear. The three of us played a game together, and very soon I forgot about naughty boys calling me rude names.

My mother always reacted like this. She never told me that I was different from other children, that I could not see as they could. And she never told me that no one in the family—neither she, my father, nor my brother, Graham—could see properly. So I grew up "seeing" things and people differently, yet not knowing there was a difference. As far as I was concerned, it was the little boys over the road who were strange and unusual, not I.

I had been born in 1946 in Beeston, Nottingham, England.

As a child, I could see a little, but not enough to recognize people or things as more than vague images coming and going in a mist of colors that were blurred and dull, as if a gauze dressing were over them. If I got very close I could see detail, but it was the kind of detail one sees when staring at a huge oil painting from only a few inches away. My mother and father were comfortable, warm shapes that I loved, but I had no picture of what their faces were really like. And the people in my dreams had no faces at all. Everything was one with the fog that had always been there from my earliest recollection, whether I was asleep or awake.

My brother, Graham, was three years older. Both of us suffered from congenital cataracts, which, in turn, caused retina damage. We inherited this disease from my father's side of the family. My mother had a different sort of eye complaint, caused by German measles when she was a child. All of us, therefore, were partially blind in varying degrees, although my father still managed to earn a living for us by working as a traveling drapery salesman.

My consciousness of home centered on things like the smell of pies baking and the crackling sound and warmth of the fire, rather than its glow. When my family sat around the table for a meal and father asked someone to pass the salt, whoever traced his or her fingers across the tablecloth in search of it often knocked over a glass or bottle. But no one ever remarked about it. It was normal. My brother and I had no inkling that such mishaps did not occur in other households.

Nor did the way we shopped at Woolworth's seem strange. I could see the toys as shapes, but I could not identify them unless I touched them. This was no doubt a problem for my mother, because the universal rule for children was always "Don't Touch!" But somehow she must have gotten the salespeople on her side so that I could feel the dolls and wooly animals and boxes of toy bricks.

One incident stands out from my earliest memories. My mother took me for the day to Skegness, a popular seaside resort for people from the Nottingham area. I was on a merry-go-round, happily whirling in my own enclosed space, and when the ride was over I sat on my painted horse and did not get off. This was because I was accustomed to my mother's coming to find me. I could never find people; instead, I always waited for them to fetch me.

So I remained on the merry-go-round. The next thing I knew, I was lifted off it by a lady with an upper-class voice. A few minutes later I was in a lost-and-found, terrified and howling the place down. After some time, through my tears, I made out a figure coming toward me. When the shape got close I knew it was a woman and I thought at first it was my "rescuer." But then, partly by her scent, I realized it was my mother. "Oh, Mom," I said, "I thought you were a lady." That phrase promptly became part of our private family language.

Why were there no attempts to have my eyes operated on? The answer is that eye surgery in those days was not as advanced as it is now, and the family had not been well served by the available methods. My brother had returned from the hospital having entirely lost the use of one eye as a result of surgery (although his remaining eye was better than both of mine put together). In turn, I had an operation, but it was not a success. My parents, particularly with Graham's experience in mind, decided against further attempts for me.

When I was five I started school, the same local private school where Graham was already a student. We were very lucky that although my father did not earn very much, he was able to afford the fees. Attending private school enabled us to bypass the state education system. Because we were Registered Blind Persons, the authorities could have required us to be sent away to a school for the blind.

I can imagine my mother saying to my father, "Whatever happens, we can't let Sheila go through what you did at a school for the blind—being shut off from sighted people and made to learn braille even though you could see well enough to be taught ordinary print. Sheila's got just enough sight to learn to read in the proper way if she holds the book close enough."

And my father, "No, we can't have her sent to a blind school. They're so rigid—even if you have some sight they won't encourage the use of it. But apart from that I don't want her to have the difficulties I had when I left school and found that after becoming used to handicapped people I couldn't cope with the sighted world."

The little school in our town of Sutton-in-Ashfield

provided the solution to these problems. Every day, as I set off from the front gate with my brother, my mother's parting words were, "Now, you two, mind how you go. And, Graham, whatever you do, don't let go of Sheila's hand." I so wanted to be free, to join the other children. But Graham would not release me. In all the helter-skelter of shouting and running feet, we walked along sedately. I hated it.

One morning I tugged so hard that I succeeded in escaping from Graham's protective hold, and I started to run. I did not get very far. With Graham shouting, "Come back, Sheila!" I ran headlong into another child and ended up crying on the sidewalk with the breath knocked out of me. So much for freedom.

In school, I gradually came to realize that the other boys and girls had an easier time of things. I knew that I had to put my face right up to a book to learn to read, but I could see the shape of Trudy, who sat next to me, holding her book away from her. Not only that, she giggled and asked, "What are you smelling your book for, Sheila?"

"I'm not smelling it, I'm reading it." More giggles, not only from Trudy, but from Malcolm, Jenny and Ian.

"You're silly," Trudy said, holding her book out at arm's length. "I can read my book like this."

So I held the book away, but the print immediately blurred. I brought it back to my face again and discovered reassuringly, that the Cat remained firmly on the Mat. "I'm not silly," I insisted.

When I returned home I went straight to my mother and asked, "Mom, why can't I hold my book out and read it like Trudy and everybody else?"

"Well," she said, "it's only that their sight's a little bit better than yours, that's all."

So I began to understand that there was something

different about me, but not—because of my parents' wise tactics—that I was in any way inferior. I did not then know that my mother had gone to see the parents of other children who attended the school to tell them about my handicap. She had asked them to explain it to their children so that the children might accept me as much as possible.

Not until I went to Trudy's for tea one day did I really come to know that I was a child apart. The television was on, and I was the only one who had to go right up to the screen to recognize the bluish glow of people and flickering objects. Trudy and her mother were sitting back on the sofa, and I could hear them laughing at the program. They said nothing to me (no doubt because my mother had been to see them) to suggest that my having to be so near the set was strange; nor did they complain that I was getting in the way of their view. But somehow I realized they were not simply following it all by sound as we did at home. That evening I did not even bother to ask my mother for an explanation.

Despite the knowledge that I was the odd one out, I still tried to do things that other children did. When I was seven, I attempted to ride a bicycle. I had a little tricycle which I rode round and round the garden, colliding from time to time with the garbage can or a wall. I was never allowed to leave the garden with it. But when Graham got a genuine junior bicycle for his birthday, I desperately wanted one as well. I plagued the life out of my parents: "*Why* can't I have a bike like Graham's? Mom, *please!*"

To this daily pleading, as to everything else, my mother would never say, "You can't have one because you can't see properly." She would invent all sorts of excuses. It was almost as if she did not want to admit even to herself that my eyesight was not right. And my father was silent because he had hoped against hope that my sight would be normal. I think he retreated into himself when he learned I had inherited his eye defect. Knowing his own difficulties, he realized that things would not be any easier for me.

Yet as far as I was concerned, all this simply added up to the fact that my brother was able to have a bike and I was not, and I didn't understand why. So one day, I "borrowed" his shiny new Hercules. I took the bike and wheeled it out of the gate into the road. There I rode it after a fashion without even realizing that traffic kept to the left-hand side of the road. It had never struck me that cars and other vehicles kept to a specific lane. But somehow, miraculously, nothing hit me, and not knowing how to stop going down a slight hill, I turned off the road, went up the curb, and slammed into a wall.

I had no idea what to do. The front wheel was flat, and the lamp bracket bent. My heart pounding, I left the bicycle where it lay and unsteadily found my way back home, where I hid upstairs for what seemed like hours.

Presently I heard voices from the kitchen. It was Graham, on the verge of tears, saying to mother, "Mom, my bike's gone. Somebody's stolen it!" Then my mother, sounding overwrought and worried, "I haven't time to think about that. Graham, have you seen our Sheila?"

At last I summoned up courage, went downstairs and told all. I cannot remember what my mother said, but she sounded relieved to know I was safe, and did not seem to care about the bicycle. But Graham was sobbing and went out immediately to recover his cycle.

Next, my father came in, and my mother told him the terrible saga. He, too, was aghast rather than an-

gry. "Sheila," he said, "whatever possessed you? You
might have been killed." Then there was a silence,
and I wondered what was coming next. At last he
spoke. "It's going to take your pocket money for a
long time," he said, "to get that bike repaired. . . ."

Very soon after this something happened to us as a
family that made Graham's damaged bicycle fade
into insignificance. My father's eyesight at last grew
so bad that he could no longer sell his drapery in the
markets around Nottingham. It was a blow that completely altered our way of life. Yet children in those
days did not enjoy the confidence of their parents
the way they do today, and Graham and I were not
told exactly what had happened. The first we knew
of a change was that one day we came home from
school and my mother asked us to help her start
packing. She said nothing about father's sudden failure to be able to earn a living anymore.

"What's happening, Mom? Where are we going?" I
asked.

"We've bought a shop," she said. "We're moving
to Nottingham."

Nottingham! This was very exciting to Graham
and me—moving to the big city away from the country town where we had lived for as long as we could
remember. We did not know, as our parents did,
that it was to be a step down in life, because our
home was to be in one of the poorest and roughest
districts of the city, St. Ann's Well Road. And what
neither Graham nor I realized at the time was that it
would be much more difficult for us to be with new
people and new children after the ones we knew and
were used to.

Instead there was simply the excitement of moving. The shop was on a corner. My mother, who
could see much better than my father, arranged the

drapery stock, marked the prices on tickets, and told
my father what they were. We were used to him
being on the road for long periods of time, but now
he was always at home and had more time to spend
with us. "Come on," he used to say, "it's time for *Jet
Morgan*." We would all sit around the radio listening, far more thrilled by *Jet Morgan* than by TV.
We could imagine him without the use of our eyes
and think of him on his adventures in space that we
would later reenact in our little back garden.

Graham and I soon found that the children in the
street were rougher than the ones we had known in
Sutton-in-Ashfield. They called us all the old names,
but as my mother had always told us to, we ignored
them. Probably because of this my brother and I
drew closer together.

Graham was a terrible bribe. I used to ask him to
read to me when we got in bed at night. And he
would say, "I'll read you a chapter of Enid Blyton if
you'll play cricket with me tomorrow." "Oh, no, not
cricket," I would protest. "You know I don't like
playing cricket." I was terrified of being hit by the
ball, which is very hard. In the end, though, lured
by Enid Blyton and her story of "Shadow the
Sheepdog," I would relent and say, "All right, I'll
have one game of cricket with you as long as you
promise not to use the hard ball." The bargaining
would then go on with Graham maintaining that it
was not really cricket if you did not use a proper
cricket ball, and me saying that I would not play unless he used a soft tennis ball. I usually managed to
persuade him to settle for cricket with a soft ball, and
he would read me my chapter.

My father also used to recite stories, making up
marvelous characters and situations. But our favorite
story was a true one, and we called it the Nottingham Station Story. "Tell us the Nottingham Station

Story," we used to beg, and with a great show of reluctance he would tell us about coming home one night on the railroad and having to change at Nottingham station and wait for his final train home.

"Well," said my father, "I went into the refreshment bar and ordered a cup of tea, and then tried to find a seat—it was very crowded you understand, about five o'clock, and everybody going home from work. But I did manage to find a seat. It must have been the only one in the whole room, and I sat there drinking my tea, and smoking a cigarette. Anyway, I finished my tea and stubbed my cigarette out in the ashtray ..."

This was the part we were waiting for, and I would say, "But it wasn't an ashtray ..." Graham used to shush me and tell me not to interrupt, and my father would say, "No, Sheila, you're right. It wasn't an ashtray. It belonged to the man next to me. It was his *jam tart*!" We used to howl with laughter. But we did not know that this was the incident that had finally convinced my father that his eyesight had deteriorated too much for him to continue going to the markets.

Fairly soon after we moved, the question of schooling came up. Although we no longer had the money to attend a private school, my mother's view had not changed. She was adamant that I attend an ordinary public school and continue to participate in the sighted world as much as possible. The Nottingham School Board disagreed. At first they tried persuasion, then a touch of heavy-handedness, and finally they threatened legal action if I were not "voluntarily" sent away to a school for the blind.

To this my mother's reply was, "Well, if I can get Sheila accepted at an ordinary public school, then she will be receiving education and that will be that. There'll be nothing you can do about it." The authorities were not pleased, but then we had a great stroke of luck. Misfortune, in a sense, came to the aid of misfortune. It turned out that the headmaster of the local junior school my mother approached was blind in one eye. He therefore had some understanding of the problem, but over and above that, he had compassion. He agreed to accept me and to see how I did. I have never stopped thanking my stars for this decision. It made a huge difference in my life, despite the difficulties.

And there were difficulties, because at that time integration was not considered the best course for blind people. The attitude was: "Either you get on without any major additional help from us, or you really will have to attend a special school." So I started at Bluebell Hill Junior School, and I remember how terrified I was at the crowds of children. There were so many more than in the school at Sutton-in-Ashfield. They all seemed to be running everywhere at once and screaming at the same time. It was as if I suddenly had access to an expected, undreamt-of mad world, and at playtime I used to sit on the wall and keep out of the way, listening to the banshee noise, seeing endless wild, moving shapes at the edge of my vision.

When I was eleven, I changed schools. I went to the Pierpont Secondary Modern, which was built at the top of a hill. By this time I walked to school on my own, and the trip there was a bit like running the gauntlet every day of my life. I would stumble over objects such as milk crates left outside the doors of houses, and I would also have to pass a crowd of boys who waited for me and jeered as I went by. Strangely, these lads had a little mongrel dog who took to me, and I to him. I used to pat the dog and make a fuss over him, and he would walk along to school beside me if the boys were not there. I think this was when I began to get the idea that in some cases animals are kinder than and preferable to human beings.

Of course there were many difficulties once I arrived in the classroom. One of the big problems I had was not being able to see the blackboard, even if I sat in the front row. One day the English mistress, Miss Pell, gave me permission to look at the board more closely. What was written was a long lesson on grammar, which was very hard to understand anyway. I had to read it a line at a time, try to remember the line, then go back to my desk to write down what I'd seen. The class got more and more fidgety and exasperated, because every time I went to the board I blocked off whole bits of the exercise that everyone else was writing down from their desks.

Fairly soon the classroom was full of cross little requests: "I'm doing that bit, Miss, can't you move her?" "She's in the way, Miss." "Miss, she's in the light." Miss Pell was very good. She told them, "Well, you'll just have to wait a moment." But the tension was building up, and after about three trips to the blackboard, I gave up, and heard frustrated protests give way to sighs of relief. The silence was broken only by pens scratching while I sat back at my desk vowing I'd rather be illiterate than go through that again. The only compensation was that I was beginning to develop a very well trained memory.

Yet for every teacher or pupil who had no consideration, there were as many who did, and these have very much remained in my mind. I remember a geography master who realized that I could not see the small print and various signs and symbols on the maps and diagrams. When it dawned on him what was happening, or rather what was not happening, he offered to coach me after school. It was thought-

ful and kind of him, and the dividend for us both
came in the exams at the end of the year when I received the second highest mark in geography. So,
given the chance, I was able to keep up with the
rest, and the question of my having to leave never
seriously arose, even though my sight was growing
increasingly worse. I managed to stay in the more advanced classes, and most of my grades were good,
particularly in subjects where the teaching was done
by lectures and I could rely on my memory. I did
especially well in history and in science, where
we had to do our own elementary experiments. I
had little difficulty remembering the terms of the
Magna Carta and the names of Henry VIII's wives;
nor, oddly enough, did I have any trouble ma-
nipulating a Bunsen burner. But with such subjects
as geography, unless I had a teacher willing to give
extra help, I was no good. At math I was quite useless because I could not follow the step-by-step instructions that were given with the aid of the
blackboard. The problems I had with decimal points
can be imagined.

I made friends at school, but not readily as other
children, mainly because I could not play the games.
I used to try to join in, but could never keep up
with the others. Although I was quite useless at tennis, I always found myself on the list for it—the bottom name. The rest of the class teamed up among
themselves, but if there was an odd number (that is,
apart from me) I would always get the last girl in
the class as a partner—in other words, by far the
worst player.

This was usually Angela, a gentle girl who became
a good friend throughout my school life. We would
play tennis together and she knew that even though
I could never hit the ball I would make the effort.

She would say, "The ball's coming, Sheila!" and I would stand there on the court in a vague sea of green, racket in the air, just praying and praying that it would connect with the ball. Perhaps once in fifty times it did connect, and in the end we resorted to a conspiracy to get us out of playing. Angela would hit the ball over the wire into the rocks beyond the court, and we would go off and spend the remainder of our gym period "looking for the ball."

When it came time for the school's Parents' Day, Miss Thompson, our science teacher, decided that the pupils would dissect flowers and then place the various parts on paper, labeling them appropriately. This was something we had been doing in biology and which, because of its intricate nature, I had not been very good at. A very considerate teacher, Miss Thompson came to me and said, "Sheila, I know you won't find it easy to do this. Would you like me to find you something else as a Parents' Day activity?"

"Yes, please," I said immediately. I had no wish to sit on the sidelines while the other students dissected their flowers and have parents look at me and think, "Oh, that must be the girl who can't see much."

Unfortunately, I did not think that what Miss Thompson came up with for me was a very good idea. On the day of the class, she said, "I've got something for you to do, and you've got a table at the back all to yourself." I went over to the table with her and she announced, "There you are. There are some empty jam jars. I want you to fill them with varying amounts of water, and then you can hit them with your pencil or pen and show what different tones and noises they make."

I was appalled. If anything would make me stand out from the rest, this would be it. "Oh, Miss," I said, "can't you find me anything different to do? Couldn't I clean out the hamsters' cages?"

She appeared a little put out and replied, "I've given this a lot of thought, Sheila. I thought it would be something you would really like to do. It's something you *can* do. You can hear it, and you can feel the water."

"Yes, Miss, but it seems so childish, especially when everybody else is doing something really important."

But I suppose she was very proud of the idea and she would not let me do anything else. So I had to fill the jars and hit them to make noises. All the while I could feel the eyes of the parents burning into me with pity I did not want.

Out of school, too, life was complicated. I had friends, including Angela, but like me they were in their teens, and at that age few young people are ready to respond to the needs of a blind friend who has to be taken around and looked after. When they were going out in the evening, I would want to go with them. But if I did go, it would mean I had to do everything they wanted to do and go everywhere they wanted to go. The sense of restriction was overwhelming, but there was no choice, because I would not go out on my own.

At dances I'd sit absolutely petrified in case a boy asked me to be his partner. I was so scared I would make mistakes or not be able to follow what he was doing. On the other hand, when nobody came and asked me, I was still on the edge of the chair with anxiety, because, left on my own, I could not see the dancers. My constant thoughts were: *What if my friends go off with their boyfriends and leave me here?* And: *No one's asking me to dance because they can see I'm blind.* I was always mixed-up and confused, and felt like a wallflower with its petals closed.

I remember one particularly terrible occasion when a boy left me standing in the middle of the dance floor after the music stopped, and I could hear everyone else moving away. I felt a sense of space opening up around me as the noise of the dancers receded to the edges of the hall. I pretended to tidy my hair but inside I was panicking until I heard someone approach. Angela had come to rescue me.

After that I gave up going to dances because it was such a trial. I had come to hate the whole business, and that cut me off from the rest of my age group, and meant that I had no opportunity at all of meeting boys. Even when I did meet them, they tended to ignore me, and naturally I worried a lot that I would never marry.

But if life was harsher than it need have been because of my stubbornness, pride and simple refusal to be considered apart from sighted people, there were compensations in living at home with parents who themselves knew the difficulties of blindness, and, more important, knew that the best way of dealing with them was not to give in. If I could not see to do something, my mother would teach me how to do it, and that was that. For example, my mother showed me a simple method of threading a needle—one that wouldn't occur to a sighted person. The method was this: Hold the needle upright (the eye end can be found because it is blunter than the point) and take the piece of thread or cotton, folded double between finger and thumb. Then push the eye of the needle down between finger and thumb, and eventually the thread will go through the eye. Success is not necessarily immediate, of course. It might take twenty attempts, but finally it always does work.

All sorts of other mechanical actions were made

possible for me by learning how to use the sense of touch. "Feel," my mother would say. This even came down to feeling where the particles of dirt were when I swept the floor, and feeling a second time, and a third, to make sure they had gone into the dustpan. It was the same with ironing clothes. The creases and folds can be felt. But, I suppose, had I been a blind child in a sighted family, I would never have been let near an iron for fear that I would burn myself. In my family, there was no alternative to making the best of one's lot.

I once asked my mother if she had had any idea before I was born that I would not have normal sight. I was appalled when she said she hadn't known one way or the other but was willing to take the risk. Seeing my horror, she then asked me whether I'd enjoyed my life so far and whether it had been really worth living in spite of the problems. Of course, I had to answer that it had. She had taken a risk, but I realized that she was right and that I still had the opportunity to live a full life in spite of my blindness—just as the rest of my family had.

During my last year at school, the decision about my future loomed large over me. What I really wanted to do was to work with dogs, because I was mad about them. On weekends I used to work at a local boarding kennel, somehow managing to cover up the fact that I could not see properly. One Saturday, I was exercising a big Alsatian in the field, and he slipped his lead. I had no idea where he had gone and was immediately gripped by panic. What if he got out and was run over? I frantically waved his lead and collar and called and called. To my astonishment and utter relief he came back. When I was interviewed by the guidance counselor, however, and told her about wanting to work with dogs, she hardly listened. The idea was dismissed as an impossibility.

Her first question amazed me. "Sheila, can you tell me where the North Sea is?"

North Sea? Apart from geography lessons I had been in person to Skegness, which is on the North Sea. But I could not answer. Moreover, I could not understand the reason for the question.

Next I was asked, "Well, then, where is Birmingham?"

That I knew. And I could answer the next question. "Can you tell me where Edinburgh is?" After giving the location of Edinburgh, I summoned enough courage to ask why she wanted to know.

"Well, if you're going to be a switchboard operator, and I'm going to recommend you, I must be sure you've got a sound knowledge of where various places are."

I was flabbergasted. Switchboard operator! It was the last job in the world I wanted. I knew that the choice for someone with my sight was restricted, but in my wildest moments I had never imagined myself condemned to plugging and unplugging calls for a living. Even so, when school ended, I found myself on the way to the Government Training Center at Long Eaton to have my capabilities as a switchboard operator assessed.

Under the eye of an extremely brusque and strict instructor I was taught the technique of working a switchboard. Then, with the Center's aid, I got a job with a big dress shop in Nottingham. I could still see enough at this stage to distinguish the lights on the switchboard, but I loathed every minute of it, and the atmosphere in the place was terrible. Yet I stuck it out for a year before moving on to a more pleasant firm where the people were friendlier.

Coming home from work one evening I had hardly closed the front door when I heard my mother call, "Is that you, Sheila? I've got some news."

"What's that?" I said, feeling for the peg to put my coat on.

"I've heard of a job that would just suit you." She couldn't wait to give me all the details, and knowing how much she worried about my going out on my own in Nottingham, I understood why she was so pleased.

The job was with a firm called Industrial Pumps. They wanted a switchboard operator. More to the point, they were not right in the middle of the city, and the journey there was much easier. I phoned the following day and got through to a Mr. Dickson. He didn't sound very encouraging at first, and my hopes began to fade when he said they had had so many applicants he did not really think he wanted to interview any more. But then I told him I was a Registered Blind Person, and his attitude changed immediately.

"Why didn't you tell me that before? Come along tonight and I'll see you. Can you make five-thirty?"

To my amazement I got the job on the spot, but only later did I learn the reason why. Mr. Dickson himself was disabled. One of his legs was shorter than the other and he walked with some difficulty. In fact, he turned out to be full of compassion, and not only on this occasion. He was a wonderful man, someone who would always listen to one's problems.

As the months went by, my eyes became gradually worse, and I came to realize how much everyday vocabulary reflects the predominance of the sighted world. The English language lacks terms to convey sensations other than sight, so blind people are not able to describe their perceptions very accurately.

The field of reference I had become used to was shrinking. Now not only words, but ideas of time and space were inexact and arbitrary, and not always those that a sighted person would form. To those accustomed to doing it, the placing of a towel on a rack or a cup on a shelf are automatic. A blind person has to think, "Six steps to the door, five paces down the hall to the bathroom." Every distance has to be worked out mentally.

By the time I was nineteen, even the blurred shapes I had always seen had vanished, had been swallowed up seemingly forever. I was able to distinguish day from night only by the slightly lighter or darker texture of the fog that had closed in on me. I could not see where I was going, either about the house or in the street. And as I could no longer read print, I had to learn braille.

It was at this point—when my range of possibilities was becoming more and more limited, when my future seemed to be an even darker vacuum—that a miracle came into my life. A new world opened up for me when I was given Emma.

2

ENTER EMMA

I was, if the truth be known, ashamed of being blind. I refused to use a walking stick and hated asking for help. After all, I was a teenage girl, and I couldn't bear people to stare at me and think I was not like them. I must have been a terrible danger on the roads. Motorists probably had seizures; suddenly coming across me wandering vaguely through the traffic, they would have to step rapidly on their brakes. Apart from that, there were all sorts of disasters that used to strike on the way to and from work.

On the evening that was to have such an effect on my life, I got off the bus just about halfway home, where I had to change buses. As usual I was walking gingerly along to the right stop. Almost immediately I bumped into something. "I'm awfully sorry," I said and stepped forward, only to collide again. When it happened a third time, I realized I had been apologizing to a lamp post. I had long since learned to put up with such idiotic things, or even to find them faintly amusing. So I carried on and found the bus stop, which was a stop at which one had to hail the bus driver. No one else was there and I had to go through the scary business of trying to figure out when the bus had arrived. Generally in this situation I tried to guess by the sound. Sometimes I would stop a large truck, and as it drew away I would stand there feeling stupid. In the end I usually managed to swallow my pride and ask someone at the stop for help.

On this particular evening I heard plenty of buses pass, or thought I did, but because I had given up hailing them for fear of making a fool of myself I let them all go by. I stood there alone for half an hour without stopping one, then I gave up. I decided to walk on to the next stop, hoping there would be people there.

I got along the pavement as best I could—and that is another frightening experience difficult to describe to anyone who has not been blind, because though you are surrounded by noise, you have no coherent mental picture of what is around you. Sometimes I could tell by the particular quality of the

sounds of traffic and footsteps that I was near buildings or passing an open space. But I had absolutely
no idea what the road might be like and still less
what might be on the other side of it. Were there
children playing, people gossiping, women buying
bread or potatoes? What did they look like? Who
were they? I could not imagine any of it. I walked
along in an enclosed gray little world, a two-foot-
square box of sounds around me.

Eventually I reached the next bus stop. But once
again there was nobody there, and no buses stopped.
So I went on to the next, and then the one after that,
and the one after that. By this time I was utterly lost
and did not know whether I was waiting at a bus
stop or a telephone pole. In the end I found myself
walking about five miles back to the terminal in the
city, because I knew if I got there I would be bound
to catch the right bus. This is what happened, but I
was between two and three hours late getting home,
and I felt pretty miserable and out of sorts when I
did get there.

I am a firm believer in Fate—it has been the
greatest single influence on my life—and I feel certain that Fate had decreed that my home teacher be
there when I finally reached home that night. Home
teachers visit the blind regularly to help, to talk over
any problems, and to supply various aids such as
braille paper, braille clocks, egg timers that ring,
and so on. Mr. Brown, who used to visit my family,
was quite a feature of life while I was growing up.
He was like an uncle to Graham and me. My mother
used to order wood, which could be bought more
cheaply through him than at a shop. When I was
young he used to bring little presents, and one of
these, a doll with several sets of clothes, I had
treasured very much.

Mr. Brown had been waiting for me for about an hour. I explained why I was so late, giving all the details of my nightmare journey. He immediately asked, "Why on earth don't you have a guide-dog?"

Those were the nine most important words of my life up to that time. Yet the suggestion was an astonishing one. The idea of owning a guide-dog had simply never occurred to me, which is strange considering my previous attachment to dogs and my hopes of finding work with them. Perhaps it was because my sight had deteriorated very gradually and I had always pretended to myself that it was not really going at all, that I could still see if I tried. I couldn't believe Mr. Brown when he suggested I should apply for a guide-dog. I imagined then that people had somehow to be very special to qualify for guide-dogs, that only a select few had them. Mr. Brown went on, "You quite obviously need a guide-dog, and you're just the right age for one."

I still could not take the idea in. Its impact was tremendous, as if someone had taken hold of the world and completely reversed its direction. "What do I do about applying?" I asked.

He replied very firmly, in a voice full of encouragement, "Well, I'll tell you. I'll get you the forms, and I'll come back with them, and we'll fill them in together. I'll do the writing for you."

When he'd gone, I sat back and thought about it. I realized it would mean I'd never again have to face the kind of terrifying ordeal that I had been through that day, blundering from bus stop to bus stop in darkness with no idea where I was. And I'd be able to go out in the evening: I could be independent!

A few days later Mr. Brown was back with sheet after sheet of questions. How tall was I? What did I do for a living? What sort of house did I live in?

What were my hobbies? They even wanted to know how much I weighed. We sent the forms off, and a reply came from the training center at Leamington Spa saying that they would send a guide-dog trainer to assess my personality and match me to a dog. I was excited, but nervous too, because at the back of my mind I was wondering, *What if they find I'm not suitable after all?* The prospect was heartbreaking.

When the trainer came, he went along with me to see where I worked and what I did. We walked together so that he could test my pace, and determine that I had no odd characteristics, such as skips and hops when I went around corners. He examined the house we lived in, which had virtually no back garden and no fencing. When I explained that we were hoping to move soon, he said, "You must have a garden well fenced off for your dog." (We did move to the other side of Nottingham.) Lastly, he told me that there was a waiting list for guide-dogs, and it would be about nine months to a year before I finally had a dog of my own.

This was in November 1965. I waited in agony to hear from the training center. Every time a letter came I seized it, and tried to find someone to read it to me as quickly as possible. During these months I had plenty of time to learn about the Guide-Dog Association. It was founded in 1934, but the original idea of using dogs to lead blind people was born in Germany during World War I, when a doctor in charge of some men blinded at the front left his German Shepherd one day to look after a soldier, and was struck by the way the dog carried out his task. The idea spread across the Atlantic and back to England. Yet, unbelievably, the use of guide-dogs was opposed here at first because people thought it unnatural, even cruel, for dogs to be put to work in this way. Fortunately, the Association flourished through a lot of hard work and voluntary effort. Today there are four centers in England for training guide-dogs and their owners.

I also learned that some blind applicants had to be rejected for various reasons, and this worried me. But the letter I wanted so much came sooner than I had thought possible. It arrived towards the end of the following May, and I had only five more weeks to wait. Would I be at the training center, Leamington Spa, on July 1? *Would I?* I was prepared to camp on the doorstep so as not to miss the day.

At last, July 1 arrived. It was, as I thought only proper, glorious weather—bright and sunny. Obviously I could not have got from Nottingham to Leamington Spa—a distance of only fifty miles, but an awkward rail journey—on my own. I was very lucky, however. I had been chatting in the office one day with one of our sales representatives, named Geoff, telling him about the prospects, and saying how wonderful it all was, but that I did not know exactly how I was going to get to Leamington. He had immediately replied, "Well, I'll tell you what, Shelia—I'll take you in my car if you like." So I was up and ready long before he called for me at nine o'clock.

As we drove along, Geoff did his best to describe the scenery to me. I disliked traveling, as there was nothing to occupy me except the business of going from point A to point B. Geoff's descriptions at least alleviated the boredom. Yet I couldn't really picture all the things he was telling me about. I had no conception of what fields looked like because I couldn't remember ever seeing one, much less a cow. I remember him saying to me, "What do you think I look like? You must have an *idea* of what I look like."

"Yes, I get an image when I hear people, just as you must imagine what people look like when you hear them on the radio. But," I added, "if you later see a photograph of what they're really like, the two images don't match up, do they?"

"No, you're right. They don't," he said.

"Well, don't blame me if I've got the wrong idea of you. . . . I think you've got dark, curly hair, and I know that you're about five-foot-seven because I can judge that when you're standing up and you talk."

"Mm," he replied, noncommittally. Then he went on, "Do you ever feel people's faces to get an image of them?" I told him I didn't, but not the reason—that it would have been like telling everyone I couldn't see.

About halfway to Leamington, Geoff asked if I'd like to stop for coffee. I didn't really want to. For one thing I wanted to get to Leamington as quickly as possible. For another, I hated going into strange places where I knew there would be lots of people, because I always felt so embarrassed. But we did stop, mainly because I thought Geoff deserved some coffee.

We turned off the highway and into a big parking lot. Geoff wanted to be helpful and he grasped my arm, not realizing how unnerving it was for me to be dragged along that way. As he was taking me from the lot, he said, "Steps here, Sheila." That was fine, as far as it went. But he didn't say whether the steps went up or down. I assumed they went up. I was wrong. I suppose I ought to have asked, to make sure. Then he led me, or more accurately, propelled me, through some doors. I got the impression we were in a very large room, full of women who were all talking. I could smell the coffee and their perfume.

Left alone while Geoff got our coffee, I panicked. I felt desperately cut off and wanted to run. Then another problem presented itself. I needed to go to the ladies' room, but I did not want to have to ask Geoff. Although the situation was not new to me, I always found it humiliating. Unfailingly, it took me right back to primary school, when I used to ask, "Please, teacher, can I leave the room?"

After a time I mentioned my predicament to Geoff. He was very good and said immediately, "Oh, of course. I'll get someone to take you." Either he didn't notice my embarrassment, or he covered up very well. He left the table and went to speak to someone. As it turned out, he must have picked the biggest and strongest woman in the room. I had bruises on my arm the next day to prove it. She got hold of me and hauled me out of my seat by brute force. "Come along, my dear," she boomed, "I'll take you. You poor thing, not being able to see." And she literally pushed me through the room.

I crashed into everything possible on the way: tables, chairs, even an occasional cup and saucer—they all went flying. I felt like a red-faced bull in a china shop. Even when I was in the bathroom, she insisted on standing guard outside the door, inquiring from time to time, "Are you all right, dear?" and "You're sure you don't need any help?" I didn't know whether to laugh or cry. I couldn't wait, once released from the grip of this Amazon, to be back in the car, driving the last lap to Leamington.

The training center, Geoff told me when we arrived, was a large, Tudor-style house, with trees all around it, standing in a great expanse of grounds. While we waited for someone to come and look after me, I had a sudden moment of misgiving. I thought, *What if I go through the course, and I can't do what-*

*ever they teach, and they say I'm not good enough to
have a guide-dog? What then?* I felt cold and alien,
and I was shaking slightly when the receptionist arrived.

She instantly dispelled my momentary panic.
"Hello, Sheila. We were expecting you around this
time. If you'd like to take my arm, I'll show you to
your room." *No pushing or dragging here,* I thought.
Geoff said good-bye, and the receptionist took me
through a lot of corridors and up several staircases.
It seemed an enormous place as she guided me
along, explaining the layout of the building, and the
way to the dining room, the lounge, the bathroom
and toilets, and so on. Then we reached my room.

"Here we are," she said. "Number Ten." She
stopped and told me to put my hand up to the door.
To my utter amazement I felt "Number Ten" in
braille. "All the doors are marked like this," she told
me, "so you won't have any trouble finding your
way." I was quite staggered. At last I was in a place
where they really understood the business of being
blind. I felt better just at the touch of the "Number
Ten" on my door. *Imagine,* I thought, as I felt the
outline through my fingers, *they actually expect you
to feel your way about.*

Then the receptionist took me into my room and
described the layout. I, of course, had to "picture" it
through my sense of touch and my estimation of the
distance between obstacles. Directly behind the door
was an easy chair and a closet. I felt along the wall
and found my bed, and along the bed to the radio
and the table. In the corner was a sink with hot and
cold taps, and on the same wall was the dressing
table. I discovered a mirror on the dressing table, and
the receptionist must have noticed my expression.
"Ah, yes," she said, "the mirror. You want to know

why. The reason is that if we don't have normal fittings such as mirrors and lamps in the rooms it would be very odd to the sighted, particularly to those who work here. We expect you to fit into a sighted world and accept these sorts of things." *Wonderful,* I thought—*integration . . .*

There was just one more item of furniture left to examine, and it was the most important. Next to the dressing table was the dog bed. It seemed massive, and I felt its innerspring mattress and blanket. It was so obviously comfortable that I fancied it myself. When I finished identifying it by touch, the receptionist said, "Well, that's it, Sheila. I'll leave you to unpack. Lunch will be in half an hour." I heard the door close behind her and started unpacking my suitcases. On the way to the wardrobe I had to keep passing the dog bed. Every time I did so I stopped and felt it. I wondered longingly what sort of dog would soon be sleeping in it.

The sound of knocking interrupted my thoughts. When I opened the door, a voice said, "Hello. I'm Brian Peel. I'm your trainer." He told me he not only trained the dogs, but also taught people how to use them. His handshake felt firm and friendly; I was sure we would get on well. "If you'd like to come down with me," he went on, "I'll show you exactly where the dining room and lounge are." We went to the lounge, and he explained the geography of the room. "We meet here each morning to begin the day's training. There are chairs around the outside. If you follow them to the right, you'll find the radio and television. On the opposite side are braille books and games. . . . Mind that coffee table. . . . If you remember that the table stands where the carpet ends, you won't walk into it."

As we went on to the dining room, the prospect of

a familiar ordeal loomed up in my mind. I hated eating meals with sighted people, since it always led to some kind of embarrassment. Sighted people usually wanted to cut my meat up and imagined it would be better if I ate with a spoon instead of with a knife and fork. Or they said, "Oh, if only I'd known you couldn't see, I would have made sandwiches." I would become so demoralized and nervous I could barely eat at all when a plate of food was eventually put in front of me. Not knowing what was on it, much less exactly where the food was, I would stab away, missing potatoes or meat or whatever, and end up bringing my teeth together on the metal of an empty fork.

At the training center it was totally different. Brian sat next to me and gave me my plate. "Here we are," he said. "Fish, chips and peas. Chips at twelve o'clock, peas at three o'clock, and fish between nine and six." So I not only knew what I was going to eat, but where to find it.

We talked during the meal. "Are there any other people here for training?" I asked.

"You're the first to arrive," said Brian. "We've three more coming this afternoon."

Then I asked the question that was burning in my mind: "When do we get our dogs?"

"In a day or two, when we know a little bit more about you and you know more about the dogs. You know, a lot of the people we get for training have never ever had a pet before they come here, and they wouldn't know how to look after a guide-dog. So first we teach the business of actually looking after a dog. Then, of course, you can't work with a dog unless you know how she's been trained, and what commands she will respond to."

"I see," I said, pausing. Then I asked, "Have you chosen the dog I'm going to have?"

"I think so," Brian answered, "but over the next two days I'll make absolutely sure. You see, I know the dogs, but I don't know the students properly yet, even though you've all filled in your questionnaires. The thing is, we match the dog to the future owner as far as possible. For instance, if an owner is young and can move quickly, we want a dog that can move quickly. If the owner's older, we want a dog that will slow down a bit. Your dog—or the one I *think* you're going to have—was puppy-walked by a woman who had no men living in the house; she's obviously a woman's dog—she gets on with them better than with men. She's quite sensitive, too, and because you've handled dogs before, we think you might suit one another. But even so, like everyone in the course, you'll have to get used to her."

After the meal we went back to the lounge and met the other students, who had arrived in the meantime. I became quite friendly with two of them, Dotty and Harry. Dotty (Dorothy, officially) was about thirty-four. She had come for her second guide-dog. Harry, a man of forty-nine who had been blinded during the war, had come for his third guide-dog.

During the afternoon, Brian began to tell us what to expect in the month ahead. He told us how he trained the dogs and how we would be trained to use them. With two people present who had already had guide-dogs, I felt like a very raw recruit. But I need not have been uneasy. Brian explained that even for people who had had a guide-dog before, it was necessary to come back to the center and retrain with their new dog. Techniques of handling were constantly being improved, and a dog had to have a month with its new owner to shift its allegiance and affection away from the trainer.

In the evening, Dotty and Harry told me about their previous dogs, and it was exciting to hear them. But when the time came to go to bed, I went upstairs to my room and felt very lonely, as this was my first extended trip away from home. In the room next to mine, I heard Dorothy's radio and decided to knock on her door.

"It's Sheila, may I come in?"

"Of course. The chair's behind the door. Sit down."

I sat down and tried to make conversation, but Dotty didn't seem very communicative. In fact, she sounded rather upset. "Would you rather I went?" I asked.

"Oh no, please don't."

So I tried to cheer her up. "Aren't you looking forward to getting your new dog? I can't wait to get mine." At this, to my amazement, she burst into tears. "Oh dear," I said, "whatever's the matter? What have I said?"

"It's all right," she sobbed. "I'll be all right. But I don't want another dog."

I was utterly at a loss. "Don't want another dog? I don't understand."

"Well," she said, "you'd understand if you'd left a dog behind." Then it emerged that Paddy, her old dog, had had to be retired early because of illness, and had gone to friends near Dotty's home. "It's so *awful*," she went on, "to have left Paddy behind and to come for another dog. I feel I've betrayed her."

I tried to console Dotty. "But if Paddy couldn't go on working, I'm sure she'll be glad to see another dog in her place . . ."

"I don't know . . ."

"But surely, for your own sake, you must try to transfer your affection."

"Yes. I know you're right. But it's easier said than done. At the moment I just don't feel able to love another dog."

There was nothing more I could do to help. I said goodnight as kindly as I could.

The next morning, all the gloom was swept away. At about half past seven I was awakened by a great chorus, not far away, of barking dogs. It was the sweetest music I had heard for years. *Which one,* I wondered lying there half-awake, *is going to be mine? Which bark is hers?* I hurried through breakfast, wanting to get down to the instruction as soon as possible. When we had assembled in the lounge, we were each issued a harness for our dogs, and, so we would get the hang of using it, there was a life-size plastic model of a guide-dog. We called him Fred.

"Your dogs," Brian began, "are used to working with experienced sighted trainers. They won't take well to your blundering around them like blind people, trying to find out where to put the harness on. This is where Fred comes in. You can practice on him first."

After we had all, in turn, found the correct end of Fred, Brian continued to instruct us on how to position ourselves by the dog. The dog was always on the left. "These exercises," Brian went on, "may seem trivial. But you will be getting a fully trained dog. The least you can do is to try to give the impression that you are a fully trained owner."

Positioned at Fred's side, I was told how to instruct him. "Let's pretend you are telling your dog to go forward. Always indicate with your right arm which direction you want. This will help the dog." My first effort was unbelievably feeble. Brian laughed. "If you were going to start off in the direction you were pointing, you'd be leaping over your dog's head. Now try again. Don't stand behind him, or you'll step on his tail." And so on. It was good that we had Fred to practice on. At least his plastic tail was not sensitive to my foot.

Our next lesson was to learn how to follow the dog. Brian played the part of the dog, because Fred had not yet been fitted with wheels. With dummy harness and Brian in the lead, we set out in the grounds of the center. I found it very difficult to follow, and to stop and go when he did. I was sure I had two left feet, and by the end of the first day's training I was convinced I would never make a guide-dog owner. But I was determined to improve, and already the feel of the harness had come to be important to me.

In the lounge after breakfast the following day, there was tremendous expectancy and excitement because we all knew we were going to meet our dogs for the first time. Brian gave us a final briefing, and then asked us to go back to our rooms. "There'll be less distraction there," he said, "and you'll get to know your dog, and vice versa, with a bit of peace and quiet."

I went up to Number Ten—now able to find my way unaided. I sat on the edge of the bed waiting, with the door open, and with enough time to have a stray, disturbing thought: *What if my dog doesn't like me? What if she growls at me?* Then I heard Brian's footsteps approaching in the corridor, and with them I heard the clicking patter of a dog's paws.

"Here we are, Sheila," said Brian as he came into the room. "Here's your dog. She's called Emma, and she's a chocolate-colored Labrador."

I heard the tail swishing the air, and Brian left, closing the door behind him. "Emma," I called. Instantly she came bounding across the room, and I was nearly bowled off the bed. Then I was licked all over. "Hello, Emma," I said. I could hardly believe it. She kept licking me, and pushing her cold nose into my hands. I knew then we were going to get along together. *She likes me,* I thought. She likes me! I could have danced around the room.

I tried to feel the shape of her head, but she would not stop bouncing up and down in front of me, twisting, turning and making snuffling noises in my hands. Every so often I got a wet nose in my face. But at last she settled down and sat by my feet, and I was able to feel what she was like. Her coat was heavy and rough, reminding me of a teddy bear's. She was smallish for a Labrador—not fat, but thickset. She had a very broad tail and ears that were as soft as velvet. And she was so lively.

Emma did not give me long to run my hands over her. She started to fetch me things. Under the dressing table I kept my shoes. She rushed after them and brought them to me one at a time. The message was quite clear: "Here I am. I'm Emma. I'm your new dog, and this is your gift, a shoe." I could not remember ever being so happy. And from those first moments of greeting, Emma's affection has never wavered. From then on she would never leave my side, and I, in turn, took on the responsibility for her every need.

3

TRAINING

My first walk with Emma took place that afternoon, and it was immediately evident why we had to have a month's training with the dogs. Although Emma obviously liked me, she would not do a thing I told her. She would obey no one but Brian. Attachment and obedience to me would come only with training and time.

I put Emma's harness on, and we started off down a quiet road near the center. Brian was standing next to us. He gave the command to go forward, but before he even got the "ward" bit out we were off, several miles down the road it seemed, and I was galloping along, hanging on grimly to the harness.

"I'll never keep this up," I managed to gasp.

"Oh, you'll soon get used to it," said Brian. "You'll grow fitter as you go along. The trouble is you've been accustomed to walking so slowly."

A guide-dog's pace apparently averages about four miles an hour. This compares with an ordinary sighted person's two to three miles an hour. What kind of speed I achieved before, I have no idea, but it was obviously not competitive even with that of the snail population. At last I began to get used to the fast rhythm and was just beginning to think I might enjoy it after all, when, without any warning whatsoever, Emma stopped. I was off the pavement before I could pull up. Emma had sat down on the curb, and I heard Brian laughing.

"Don't go without your dog—that's lesson number one," he said. "If you go sailing on when she stops at the curb, you'll get run over. She stops, you stop."

"Well, I didn't know she was going to stop, did I? And you didn't tell me."

"No, you're right. But you've got to learn to follow your dog."

Brian was about twenty-eight, a very pleasant man who had a great sense of humor. I imagined him as good-looking, with fair hair and glasses. I liked him especially because he refused to make concessions to our blindness. He expected us to be independent. Rather than mop us up and say, "There, there," when we fell off the curb, he would turn it into a joke, which was the best medicine. At least it was for me. It certainly made me get up and think, "I'll show you who can be a good guide-dog owner."

So on this occasion, I got back behind Emma, took up the harness again and asked, "What next?"

"You've got to cross this road. First you listen for any traffic. If it's quiet, you give Emma the command to go forward."

When I could hear no traffic, this is what I did. But nothing happened.

Brian said, "She knows that you're behind her, not me. You've got to encourage her, to make her want to take you over the road."

"Good girl, Emma," I said, "there's a clever dog." After a little more of this persuasion and the word "Forward," thrown in from time to time, she finally took me across the road.

Crossing a road with a guide-dog is a matter of teamwork: Whatever you do, you do it together. I have met sighted people with such weird ideas about this. Either they think the dogs are not very clever,

but just wear the harness to show their owner is
blind—a sort of plea for help—or they think the dogs
are superhuman and the blind people idiots who are
being taken for a walk the way other people take
their dogs. The importance of partnership, or even
its existence, never seems to occur to most people.
My job when crossing a road was to listen, and
Emma's was to look. Only when I could hear nothing was I to give her the command to cross. But if I
was wrong in my assessment of the traffic, and she
could see something coming, she would wait until it
was clear.

Guide-dogs are taught to stop and sit down at every curb and wait for the next command. The four
basic commands are, "Right," "Left," "Back,"
and "Forward." And you have to position yourself
with your dog so that you give her every opportunity
to obey the right command. It is also important to
keep talking to the dog, and Brian reminded me of
this on our first walk, just after we had crossed the
road.

"Don't stop talking, or Emma'll think you've
fallen asleep."

"What do I say?" I asked rather stupidly.

"It doesn't matter, as long as you make it interesting. Tell her what you had for breakfast, if you
like."

So there I was, running along a street in Leamington discussing bacon and eggs with a chocolate-
colored Labrador. Brian went on, "You're working
together, and if you stop talking, she'll stop working.
You've got to keep her interest. She's a dog, and
there are lots of nice, interesting smells all around,
and things passing that you can't see. So unless you
talk to her, she'll get distracted, and stop to sniff a
lamp post." I was quite hoarse by the time we had
finished our first walk together.

I owe a great deal to Brian, not only for his training, but also for matching Emma and me together. His assessment of all he knew about us resulted in an inspired pairing, as time was to prove.

One day I remember asking him where Emma came from. What I really meant was, "How do the centers come by the guide-dogs?" Brian explained that they came to Leamington, or one of the other centers, after being puppy-walked. The Guide-Dog Association has a big breeding and puppy-walking center near Warwick. It owns a number of brood bitches and stud dogs that are boarded out to people as pets, because, naturally, a permanent kennel life is not desirable, and living with a family is a much happier arrangement. At the same time the Association controls which dog mates with which. When the litters come along, it picks the dogs required for training. At about eight weeks old, a puppy undergoes various tests to see if it is basically bold and friendly, and capable of being trained as a guide-dog.

Dogs bred in this way form about sixty per cent of the total, and there are now about two thousand guide-dog owners in England. The remaining forty per cent of the dogs come to the Association either by purchase or donation from breeders or private individuals. But the rejection rate is high. Dogs are kept on approval for about three weeks to see if they are suitable. If they're not, they're returned to their owners. The dogs chosen are usually female, because the male dog has a rather different outlook and nature, including a territorial instinct, and is not as tractable as the female, who is spayed for the purposes of being a guide-dog. About seventy per cent of the breeds used are Labradors, like Emma— though I prefer to think she is unique, even among Labradors—and the remainder are German Shepherds, collies, golden retrievers, and crosses from all of these.

Once the selection is made, the puppies go to people called puppy-walkers, who live around the training centers, and give homes to potential guide-dogs for about a year. In this time they have to teach the dogs the basics—to be well-mannered and clean in the house, to keep off furniture, not to beg for food, and to obey commands such as "Sit," "Stay," "Down," "Come," and so on. The dogs are taught to walk on a lead, but not at heel, because of course they will eventually be required to walk in front of a blind man or woman.

In general, the puppy-walkers are expected to take the dogs everywhere with them so that they are not shy of traffic, buses or trains, or the sort of sudden noises that sometimes occur in the street, such as pneumatic drills. The puppy-walkers are also specifically instructed to take the dogs shopping. During this phase the puppies grow up and become used to urban life, and at the same time should remain bold and friendly.

At this point, Brian told me, they come to the centers for guidance training, which lasts about five months. The puppy-walkers do a wonderful job. I couldn't do it myself: Have a dog for a year, then part with it; then have another, and see it go, and so on. I really admire those who do so much to forge the first essential link between dog and blind person.

Naturally, when Brian told me all this, I wanted to know who had puppy-walked Emma. He said, "Someone named Paddy Wansborough. She's a marvelous woman. She's given nine or ten dogs to the Association after puppy-walking them."

I determined that when I got home I would contact Paddy Wansborough.

The following day, I was out with Emma again.

As the training progressed I gradually grew accustomed to her. We used a minibus to get us about Leamington and this played a big part in the training because we learned how to use public transportation. When we were on the bus and the dogs were under the seats, I heard a great bellow from Brian, "I can see two brown paws sticking out." *Brown paws*, I thought, *that must be Emma.*

He went on. "Do you want somebody to step on her?"

"No, of course I don't."

"Well, do something about it."

I began to wonder if my first impression of Brian had been wrong. But though he was shouting at me a lot, he must have guessed what I was thinking.

"No one else is going to tell you these things, Sheila. If you don't learn them here, Emma'll be the one that suffers, not you."

My trust in Emma grew daily, but I really knew she had transferred her affections from Brian to me on the tenth day of my stay at the center. Up to then, she had always slept until morning in her dog bed on the other side of the room. But on this particular evening, she refused to go to her bed. Instead, she curled up on the floor as near to my pillow as she could get. I felt then that we had made it. We were a team, each needing the other's company.

I woke the next morning with an odd sensation. It felt as if there was a steamroller on my chest. Emma was sitting on top of me, pushing with her nose, telling me, I have no doubt, that it was time for us both to get up. She was full of exuberance and could not wait to start the day. When I did get up, I could hear her shake herself in anticipation, and stand wagging her tail near the door.

One of the center's ingenious ways of familiarizing us with the day's program was by using tactile maps.

Pavements, buildings, and so on were raised on a wooden map of Leamington, so we could feel our way over the routes beforehand, right down to the pedestrian crossings and the bus stops. Emma would find these things for me, but I had to be on the right road, and the map helped enormously to ensure that we did not lose our way.

Our walks grew more complicated, and Brian would try to find places where there was construction, to satisfy himself that we had mastered the feat of getting around it, as well as other obstacles. Bus trips and shopping expeditions were also in the curriculum, and I really enjoyed shopping with Emma. She would not only find the shop, but also take me up to the counter. I began to forget I was blind. No one fussed around me any longer. They were all too interested in Emma.

But things did not always go smoothly. I was not keen on the obstacle course we had to practice. Emma reacted very quickly, and usually I was not fast enough to follow. She would see the obstacle, assess it, and make a snap decision which way to go. Before I knew what was happening she would have changed course to one side or the other, and I would be left in a trail of harness and confusion. Brian always seemed to be on hand when I made mistakes, even when I thought he was following some other student. I would hear a great shout, "When your dog jumps, you jump."

It was easier said than done. On occasions like this, Emma would lose confidence and immediately sit down. It was almost as if she were saying, "It's no good me doing my part if all you can do is to trail behind and finish up in a heap." The only way I could get her back to work again was literally to apologize and promise to do better next time.

It was while we were doing the obstacle course

one time that I learned one of Emma's aversions. Suddenly Emma shot off like a rocket, and I felt myself being taken at right angles up a steep grass bank. As we went, I heard Brian hysterical with laughter. When we finally came to a stop, I said rather breathlessly, "What was all that about? Whatever did she do that for?"

"Oh, it's Napoleon."

"Napoleon? What do you mean, Napoleon?" I thought Brian had suddenly gone out of his mind.

"You know," he said, "the cat. Napoleon the cat."

"Oh," I said. But I still did not know why Emma had shot up the bank.

Brian, still laughing, explained that Emma could not stand cats. She knew better than to chase them, but if she saw one she would take off in the opposite direction. Brian congratulated me on my alacrity in following and promised to keep us in mind if there was ever a guide-dog expedition to Everest. At the same time, I thought that the only way to cure Emma of her dislike of cats would be to get one, and I put that on my list of resolutions for when I got home.

That evening as we were sitting in the lounge, Brian came in and we laughed again about Emma and the cat. Then I asked him something that fascinated me more and more the longer the course went on. How were the dogs trained to accomplish the amazing things they did for us? It is a fairly simple matter to train a dog to sit at a curb, but how were they trained to disobey us? I asked Brian, "For instance, I told Emma to go forward yesterday when I hadn't heard a car coming, and she wouldn't go because she'd seen one. How on earth do you train them to do that?"

Brian replied, "Once you've got a dog basically trained, and you're waiting to cross the road, you see a car coming and tell the dog to go forward. The dog, naturally, obeys immediately, but you don't move, and the car—other trainers drive them for these exercises—honks, and makes a lot of noise, and the dog comes back on the pavement. By repetition of this sort of thing it is conditioned to associate the moving vehicle with danger, and therefore, despite all instinct to obey, refuses to move even when the command is given. Of course, only fairly intelligent dogs will respond like this, and that's why we have to be very stringent with our tests of character and aptitude to begin with."

"What about obstacles?" I asked.

Brian explained that the principle behind teaching dogs not to walk with their owners into obstacles is to get the dog to associate an obstacle with displeasure—to use a mild word—and also distress. A start is made with something simple, like a post. The dog walks the trainer into the post, is immediately stopped, the post is banged to draw attention to it, and then the right way of proceeding, allowing room, is shown. The next time a forceful *"No"* is shouted when the trainer collides with the post, and the right way is shown again. So by repetition the dog eventually gets the message, and at the same time, the range of obstacles is extended to include the most frequent pavement obstacles of all—people.

It sounded simple in a way, but I knew a lot of work and talented training went into all this. The trainers, Brian told me, worked with a blindfold when they felt the dogs had reached a certain standard of proficiency. They did this for about two weeks to create real working conditions for the dogs and give them confidence through working with someone they knew.

It was interesting to hear Brian explain it all, particularly in the light of what followed in the last stage of the course, the disobedience part. We were nearing the end of our month at Leamington, and went out once more in the minibus. By now, Emma's paws were always well tucked away. Brian told us we were going to the railway station as a final test.

I had always loathed railway stations because of the noise, the hundred and one different obstacles and the general sense of bustle which, if you are blind, is frightening. I would never go into one, even if there were a sighted person to take me. But Brian was adamant. "You've got to get used to it. You might want to go by rail one day or meet somebody at a train, and you've got Emma to guide you now. She knows her way around. It's easy."

I was not convinced. We arrived at the station, and I put Emma's harness on. Brian told me he was going to park. "You go in; Emma knows the way. I'll be with you in a minute or two."

Emma took me through the doors, down a couple of flights of steps, in and out between people on the platform, and sat down. I had no idea where I was. I just stood and waited for Brian. When he came over to me he said, "Emma's sitting bang on the edge of the platform. There's about a six-foot drop in front of you to the railway line. Now tell her to go forward."

I was petrified. "You must be joking," I said.

"No, go on. Tell her to go forward."

I stood still, not knowing what to do. This really was a terrible test. Dare I do it? In that moment I really did not want a guide-dog. Everything I had heard about them, all the training we had done, all I felt about Emma flashed through my mind, and it meant nothing. I just wanted, then and there, to lay the harness handle on Emma's back and leave, get out, escape, anything. But, in a sort of hoarse whisper, I heard myself saying, "Forward."

Immediately, she got up, and almost in the same motion pushed herself in front of my legs. Then she started pushing me back, away from the edge of the platform.

I have never felt so ashamed in all my life. How could I possibly have been so doubting, so unworthy of Emma? Brian said, "There you are. I told you Emma would look after you, whatever you do. Whatever you tell her to do, if there's any danger in front of you, she'll push you away.

So that was it. We had made it. The sense of freedom was overwhelming. I got over my awful feelings of guilt, because I sensed that Emma understood and forgave. That afternoon I walked with her down the busy main road in Leamington, crowded with shoppers. I walked with a great big smile on my face, weaving in and out of all those people, thinking, *I don't care if you can see I'm blind. I can see too. I've got Emma, and she's all I need.*

4

HOME AGAIN

All too soon the day came when we were going to go home, Emma and I. It happened to be raining—pouring down—and the weather matched my mood. Even though I could not see the rain, I felt very gray and depressed. I hated the idea of having to leave the center and all the friends I had made. Even more, I really did not want to go home, although I now had Emma, and I kept trying to convince myself that things back in Nottingham were *bound* to be different. I was afraid that somehow I might be enveloped in the old ways again. I had not yet grasped to what an enormous extent Emma was about to change my life. I still had to learn to put my confidence in her.

Heavy with misgivings, I left Leamington with Emma on her harness beside me. The two of us arrived in Nottingham by train, were met and taken home. Once there, I let Emma off the lead and took off her harness. She went wild. Everyone was instantly entranced with her. She bounded all over the place, through every room, round and round. I could hear her tearing about, sending rugs flying, stopping to sniff each chair and table leg. The air swished to the wagging of her tail and resounded with her snortings and sniffings. This, she obviously realized, was where she was going to live.

She was such a different Emma from the sober, responsible animal on the harness, and for the first time I appreciated that there were two distinct sides to her character: one when she was working and in charge of me, and the other when she was off the harness, totally joyous, full of fun and energy and as far from any sense of responsibility as a clown. My misgivings began to evaporate.

The first night back, Emma slept at the bottom of the bed. She had decided that there was no other place good enough for her, and in the morning she woke me with her usual insistence. It struck me that this morning we were really starting a new life together. We would be going out into Nottingham on our own. I jumped out of bed and started dressing. This was not my usual form, because I'm a very slow, sleepy starter, but on this day of all days I

could not wait to find out how Emma and I, put to
the test, would do together.

Over breakfast I decided we would go to visit
some old friends, Norman and Yvonne, whom I used
to visit when my sight was better and who lived
quite nearby. They were customers from the days of
the St. Ann's Well Road shop and would, I hoped,
be pleasantly surprised.

I had the directions worked out in my mind after
a telephone consultation. They presented no problems: All I had to do was to go out of our front gate,
tell Emma to turn right at the top of the road (a
main road), turn right again, go straight to the bottom, turn left, and ask Emma to find the first gate.
So, off we went.

Twenty minutes after setting out, we were standing on the porch of Norman and Yvonne's house, and
I was feeling for the bell. We had done it. To anyone
walking down that Nottingham street, there may
have appeared nothing out of the ordinary about a
girl and a dog standing in a doorway waiting for the
bell to be answered. But inside me was a huge sense
of triumph: It was a milestone. "Good girl, Emma,"
I kept saying. I was so proud of her.

Norman and Yvonne were delighted to see me
and they were even more thrilled to meet Emma.
They made a great fuss over her. Several hours later
we set off for home and found our way back to the
main road. Then came a terrible realization. In my
excitement, I had forgotten to count how many in-
tersections we had crossed. There had been no need
to count on the way because we walked as far as the
road went, up to a T-junction. But I should have
counted for the return trip. And I hadn't. So there I
was with no idea where I should tell Emma to turn
left. After a whole month of training, I had right

away forgotten one of the cardinal principles: Always count the roads as you go.

What could I do? I thought: *There's no trainer now to save me.* Emma, all unknowing, was taking me along at her furious pace, in what I feared was an endless race to nowhere. Not only that, but I felt I had let her down.

Emma wasn't in the least daunted, however, and, ignoring my commands, started taking me down a side road. I tried to stop her. "No, Emma. No! Go back, go back." But she paid no attention. In turn, I dared not let go of her, so I had to follow. At last she turned left again and sat down. Instinctively I put my hand out. I felt leaded lights and painted wood with one or two blisters. It was my back door. If I had forgotten to count the roads on the way out, Emma certainly hadn't!

Not long after we were home from Leamington I wrote to Paddy Wansborough, the woman who had puppy-walked Emma. By "wrote" I mean that I sent a tape-recorded cassette to tell her how much Emma had come to mean to me, and to thank her for giving Emma as a guide-dog after puppy-walking her. That was the beginning of a correspondence by cassette, and of a friendship that continues to this day.

Through this correspondence I learned all sorts of little details about Emma. Paddy had her from the age of eight weeks and she sent me a photograph taken at this time. Although I had to rely on other people's descriptions of the photograph, it was splendid to have a picture of Emma as she was when she was first picked out of the litter to be a guide-dog. She was already eighteen months old when I first met her, so of course I missed all her puppy ways, but to hear Paddy describe them on cassette was the best possible substitute. She said that Emma had always been a busy dog, was interested from the beginning in doing things constructively, and always gave the impression of having something on her mind. This confirmed what I knew of her.

On one cassette Paddy told me a story that I possibly found more amusing than she had at the time. One day Paddy planted some hundred and fifty bulbs in her garden. She had then gone indoors, leaving Emma still playing on the lawn. After about half an hour, Emma came in looking extremely pleased with herself. When Paddy happened to glance out the window a moment or so later, she was confronted with a huge pile of bulbs neatly stacked on the back doorstep. Emma had dug each one up with loving care and immense energy, and was thrilled to have been such a help in restoring them to their owner.

Before long, Paddy asked me to visit her in Yorkshire. Through our cassette correspondence, I felt I already knew her, but I wondered if Emma would remember her for her owner. As we got off the train, I heard Paddy's voice greeting us. "Hello, Sheila. How are you?" It was the signal for Emma to go berserk. She leaped all over Paddy, but although she was delighted to see her again, she kept coming back to me as if to say, "I'm pleased to be here, but I haven't forgotten that I'm your dog."

Emma and I went to my job at Industrial Pumps together as soon as we were settled again. At that time I lived and worked on opposite sides of Nottingham. I had to catch two buses, with a walk across the Market Square in the middle of the city in between. The terminal for the first bus was at the bottom of our road, so that part was easy. Emma trotted down the road with her tail in the air; I could feel it brushing my hand as we went along. I began to learn then how sensitive I was able to be, via the harness, to what she was doing. Through it I could tell whether her ears were up or down, whether she was turning her head left or right and all sorts of little movements.

We found the stop easily, and from that moment Emma loved going on buses. It was not just the bus itself, however. One important factor was the admiration she always received: "Oh, what a lovely dog. Oh, what a beautiful color." And so on. I could sense Emma basking in the glory. She had picked the second seat on the right for me. For some reason, this was the place she chose every time on this particular bus. I sat down, and Emma crawled under that seat.

After we had been going to work together for about three weeks, we were nearing the bus one morning when I heard a commotion going on inside it. As we came alongside I could hear a woman's muffled shout, "You'll have to get up, you know. You can't sit there. I tell you it's Emma's seat. Come on—they'll be here in a minute."

On other buses, Emma simply went for any empty seat, preferably—in the winter at least—one near the heaters. But since we normally traveled in the rush hour, the buses, apart from our first one, were very often full. So Emma had to use a different technique. She would drag me along the aisle, nosing everyone else out of the way if there were standing passengers, decide on where she wanted us to sit, and then stare at whoever was sitting there until he gave way. People usually gave the seat up very quickly before the bus was in an uproar. This, of course, appealed to the exhibitionist in Emma. When she was sure she had her audience, she would turn to me, lay

her head across my knee, looking, I imagined, quite
devoted and possibly a little pathetic. By this time
the entire bus was hers.

That first morning, when I walked into the office,
there was a reception committee waiting. While my
coworkers greeted me, they were clearly more interested in seeing what Emma was like. Emma once
again responded with great delight, and when I had
taken her harness off, she took it around, her tail
wagging, to show everyone in turn.

So she was an immediate hit. After the others had
gone, she inspected her basket, played for a while
with a rubber toy I had brought with me to occupy
her, then settled down. The telephone had already
started ringing, and soon it was like old times—with
the tremendous difference of that reassuring sleeping
form under my desk.

During my lunch hour I took Emma out of the office for a run in the local park. This was something I
had decided I must do every day. Since she worked
hard it was only fair that she should have a free run
whenever possible. I sat myself on a bench with my
sandwiches, let her off the lead, and she went charg-
ing across the grass. I soon heard barking in the distance and recognized Emma. But every so often she
would come back to me, touch my hands with her
nose, and then scamper off again. It was something
that she never failed to do whenever we went to the
park from then on.

The first week went by very happily. Traveling to
and from work, in fact, became easier every day. I
did not have to give Emma all the directions in the
Square because she soon began to take me straight to
the correct road and across to the bus stop. I soon
discovered that Emma had only to take any route
once and she knew it. But I also found there was a
drawback in having such an intelligent dog.

About the middle of the second week we set off for work as usual. I merely said to Emma that we were going to the office. We caught our first bus, and reached the Market Square. Everything was fine. But when we got to the first road to cross in the Square, Emma sat down instead of going forward. I listened for traffic, and when I thought it was clear, I told her to go forward. But she would not move. She simply continued to sit.

I could not understand what was going on. I thought that perhaps I had misjudged the traffic, so when it was quiet I told her again. Still she would not go straight ahead. Instead, she stood up and turned right, taking me along the pavement. "Emma," I said, rather desperately, as I was being dragged along, "where are you taking me? Where's the bus stop? Come on. Bus stop . . ." But no, she would not listen, or if she did listen, she certainly did not take any notice.

We went on, crossed a road, made a sharp left turn, and crossed another road. Then she sat down again. I had no idea where we were. I had completely lost my sense of direction and was utterly confused about the pattern I had to keep in my mind in order to reach the bus stop. I was not only disappointed in Emma, but slightly upset and annoyed with her as well. "Emma," I said crossly, "we shall be late for work." How do you tell the boss that it was the dog who made you late?

Reluctantly, I decided to appeal to a passerby. "Excuse me," I said as the next footstep approached, "can you tell me how to get to the number forty-three bus stop, please?" There was a silence for a second or two, during which time I thought: *No one knows where it is.* We are really lost. Then a man's voice, obviously puzzled, said, "Forty-three bus stop?

You're *at* the forty-three bus stop. Your dog's at the foot of the post." I was relieved, astonished, and utterly baffled. We got on the bus when it came along, and I put the incident out of my mind——until the following morning.

This time Emma went left instead of right, crossed another road, turned right, crossed a further road, walked along, and sat down. We were at the forty-three bus stop again. I was unnerved, but by now I'd gotten used to the feeling. At work, I asked Carol, a friend who I knew came to the office via the Market Square, if there was any construction on the route I had originally mapped out. She said no, and that there was no new building or any kind of obstruction.

I was at a loss. I thought and thought, and then the only possible explanation came to me: Emma, having learned a route, became bored with having to follow it every day. So she invented variations. From then on she found a series of routes around the Market Square quite independently of any guidance from me, and chose one of them every day. I soon became resigned to this and got up ten minutes earlier just to allow for Emma's possibly making a mistake. But, of course, she never did.

5

ANITA

By now I was learning that Emma gave me a certain freedom not only to go where I liked but also to do what I liked. I decided to enroll in an evening class called Writer's Craft. It was through this that I met Anita.

During one of the breaks at the class I heard a warm, friendly voice saying, "Do you mind if I talk to your dog? I've never met a guide-dog before. She really is a gorgeous color. And isn't she clever? I saw the way she brought you across the road this evening. It was amazing."

Amazing? Why amazing? I had really been thinking to myself that Emma had not been at her most cooperative. She certainly did not cross the road where I had wanted her to. Perhaps this girl had the answer. "What did she do, then?" I asked.

"Oh, don't you know? Well, there is construction right along the street—I think there's a burst water pipe—and she wouldn't bring you over the road by the crossing because there's a trench there. Instead I saw her look around, take you to the traffic lights up the road, wait for them to turn green, and then bring you across there, beyond the trench."

So that was it! I gave Emma a pat on the head, and said, "Good girl." Her response was a sort of snort that seemed to say, "Well, thank goodness someone's told you. You needn't have been impatient with me, you see."

The owner of the voice, which had a strong Yorkshire accent, eventually introduced herself as Anita. And this was the start of a very true friendship—all because of Emma. Anita was nineteen, the same age I was, and she had come to take a job in Nottingham. I gathered later that she was attractive and had a good figure and short, dark hair. As the weeks went by I came to look forward to meeting her at the classes. She was interested in writing short stories, and I was trying to write poetry. We always chatted at the break, and one night I asked her what she did on the weekends.

"I go back to Hull quite a bit," she said, "but this coming weekend I'm going horseback riding."

Horseback riding! My heart skipped a beat. It was something I had always yearned to try, something I had heard so much about from girlfriends. But my mother had always resolutely forbidden it. In my mind I could hear her words, "Certainly not, Sheila. No, I won't entertain the idea for a minute."

But now Anita's mention of this forbidden activity gave me a thought—and my mother never need know. "Horseback riding," I said. "How marvelous. Would you take me?"

From the tone of her voice Anita was obviously very surprised. "Take you? Would you really want to, Sheila? I mean, wouldn't you be scared? I mean . . . because you can't see properly?" This was a reaction I was not prepared for, strange as it may seem. I had never thought of my blindness as an obstacle. "Never even thought about it," I said.

"Well," said Anita, "I'll book a ride for you too. I'll phone you at work tomorrow."

I awaited Anita's call with some excitement. But it was not until the afternoon that the phone rang, and

Anita's voice betrayed that something had gone wrong. "Sheila, I don't know how to say this. I've been in touch with the stable, and a half a dozen others as well. They won't take you. They all refused point-blank. . . . I'm afraid it's because you can't see."

There was a pause while I let this sink in. Then she added, "And I've canceled my ride as well."

"Oh, Anita," I said, "why did you do that?"

"Because if they won't have you, I don't want to go either. Why should they discriminate just because you can't see?"

Anita's kindness lightened my gloom at the thought of no one accepting me. The gesture was typical of her—warm-hearted and unselfish. Even so, I felt guilty about spoiling her weekend and said so.

"No, Sheila," she said. "It doesn't matter a bit. Anyway, we'll get you on a horse somehow, even if it means trying to pretend that you can see."

The switchboard buzzed again within minutes. It was Anita, with a triumphant note this time in her no-nonsense voice. "I've booked rides for both of us."

I was thrilled. And apprehensive. "How are we going to do it. How can we hide the fact that I can't see? They're bound to notice, and then you'll get into hot water. And something else: What about Emma? They'll know she's a guide-dog because of her harness."

"Leave it all to me," said Anita. "We'll think of something. And I'm sure we can get someone to look after Emma and hide her harness."

I could not get over Anita's persistence. She was doing all this just for me. When the weekend came I put on a sweater, and, because I had no proper riding gear, my oldest slacks. They were the subject of critical comment from my mother, but I prudently let the subject rest. Emma and I met Anita as arranged, and as we took a bus to the stable, she told me what she had planned.

"I've got it all worked out. We're going to meet a friend of mine who will take charge of Emma's harness just outside the stables. Then we'll link arms and get you to your horse, and I'll make it clear that I'm helping you up because you've never ridden before. When you get up on your horse, I'll tell you what to do, and we'll keep talking to one another all the time after we set off, so you'll know exactly where I am."

It sounded fine. But I could not help feeling a slight panic already stirring in me. At the same time I knew I could not back out. I thought, *I must bluff it for Anita's sake.*

We met Anita's friend and gave her Emma's harness, while Emma herself accompanied the three of us on a lead. Then, in the stable yard, the tight feeling inside gripped me. I could hear all sorts of voices. I felt sure someone was going to come up and say, "You can't see! What are you doing trying to ride one of our horses?"

But everyone was too busy with his own mount to bother with me, and I was heaved up onto the back of my horse, after some fumbling for the stirrup. A-nita had brought him to me, and said he was named Rocky. I sat up on his back, feeling very strange and hissed, "Now what do I do? Anita, what do I do?"

"Don't worry," came the reply as I heard her alongside me. "Give me your hands. This is how you put your fingers and thumbs around the reins. Like that. That's it. No, thumbs outwards. That's it. Now hold on, and when we're ready to go, just gently dig your heels in his flanks ... not too hard ..."

So we moved along, and I heard Anita just behind me, keeping up a running commentary: "Isn't that a fantastic old oak tree? . . . What's Rocky like,

Sheila? . . . He's very Roman-nosed, isn't he?
. . . Isn't that lovely down there? . . ." And so
on, in order to keep me reassured of her presence.

All went well, and I was feeling quite relaxed as
we trotted gently along. I was imagining that I was
Maid Marian in Sherwood Forest sedately riding to
meet Robin Hood, when suddenly something must
have frightened Rocky. He half-reared, then took off
with me at a brisk canter. I was petrified. I dropped
the reins and grabbed the saddle and hung on.

The wind rushed by my face. I heard Anita
shouting, "Pull your reins back. Sit back in the
saddle." All her instructions were to no avail. I was
carried on helplessly, as never before through my
daylight world of darkness, bumping up and down,
just hanging on, powerless in the wind and sound of
hooves.

Then, as capriciously as he'd started, Rocky slackened his pace. He came to a halt and put his head
down, and I heard him tearing up grass, chomping it
in his teeth. But that was all the sound there was. A
new fear set in. I had completely lost my sense of
direction. I should never have done it. I thought,
*Now they're bound to find out I'm blind. And they'll
blame Anita.*

At that moment I heard hooves again, and Anita's
voice, "Go on, Sheila, make him move. Dig your
heels in, don't just sit there." At last, after some
prodding and persuasion and more advice from Anita, we got Rocky to move. When we returned to the
stable, no one even suspected that I was blind. All I
overheard was, "Trust Rocky to take off like that.
Rather her than me. I reckon she did well to stay
on."

We had got away with it! And, despite the sensa-
tional behavior of Rocky, I had to admit that I had

enjoyed it, and from then on, when we could, Anita and I used to go horseback riding together.

One day, after we had been riding, Anita invited me back to her apartment. While we were drinking tea, Anita suddenly said, "You know, I don't very much like this apartment, Sheila. It's terribly small and cramped. I'd love something bigger, but everything's so expensive. I went to a lovely apartment the other day. It was fabulous—big sitting room and separate bedroom. Not like here, where you have to make the bed do for a sofa during the day, and where the kitchen's no bigger than a cupboard. If I could get someone to share with me, then I might be able to afford it. But I suppose it's all a dream—like getting my short stories published!"

We both laughed. But her remarks had planted a seed in my mind. I had already decided that I would like to go out into the world and be independent, now that I had Emma to guide me. At home I did my share of the household tasks, and I knew I was capable of doing the same elsewhere. Yet, independence had never been more than a dream.

What would Anita say if I suggested that I might be the one to share with her and solve her problem? I deliberated for a moment and said, "How about sharing an apartment with me?"

Her reaction was more than I had dared hope for. "Oh, Sheila, what a terrific idea!"

But I thought I had better find out if she realized all the implications. "Do you *really* think it would be a good idea? What about Emma, for instance?"

"Well, you couldn't come without Emma. I just took that for granted."

"Ah. What I really mean is . . . doesn't the fact that I can't see put you off a bit?"

"Put me off? No, of course not. You get along at

home quite well. Why shouldn't you do the same sharing with me?"

It was a tantalizing, enormous idea. Yet I did not want Anita to rush into something she might regret and, to be honest, it would mean so many changes in my life that I thought we should not decide there and then. I suggested we consider the whole business overnight. Anita agreed, but as she saw Emma and me to the door she said, "I'm certain I know what the answer's going to be."

There was, however, a possible complication that I had forgotten to mention during our exciting discussion: Tiss. Tiss was my ginger cat. As I said, one of the first things I had wanted to do after I got Emma home from Leamington was to buy a kitten, in the hope that she would gradually overcome her dislike of cats. We went to the local pet shop, and after the man had described all the kittens he had, I thought a ginger tom sounded the nicest. So this warm, tiny bundle of fur was removed from its cage and placed in my hands. I felt Emma put her nose up to him. She did not run a mile, and he did not spit at her. So he was the one. He was lovely, but grew into a strange cat.

He was so silent about our house that I could never hear where he was, and I feared treading on him until I bought him a collar and a little bell. But he soon learned how to move without tinkling the bell. Tricks apart, he seemed to worship Emma, and despite the dislike she had always shown for cats, she made an exception for Tiss. He in turn would never go to sleep without Emma, and this he did by curling up on top of her in the dog bed. Tiss, therefore, was a major consideration when it came to deciding about moving into a flat with Anita.

First, however, I had to broach the idea to my mother. She worried about me anyway, so I did not anticipate an overenthusiastic reaction. Yet I hoped she would approve because one of her great beliefs was that blind people should be part of the sighted world as far as they could. She was washing dishes when I explained the plan to her, and, partly because she was hard of hearing, and partly because of the noise of suds and pots, I thought at first she hadn't heard me. Then she said, "Are you sure you want to do this?"

"Yes, Mom, quite sure."

"Well, I mean, are you certain you'll be able to manage? It's a big break."

"Yes, I'm certain I can do it. And it really is a chance to be independent."

She was silent again, and I sensed that she was torn between natural maternal anxiety and wanting me to put into practice what she had always taught me.

"Do you think Anita will really understand the problems?"

"Yes, I'm sure she will. Anyway, she never mentions eyesight. She's wonderful."

At that moment Graham came in from work. He had a job as a piano tuner, although his great passion was playing the guitar. When we had explained what I was proposing, he said, "I think it's great. Anita sounds okay—but in any case you'll cope, won't you, Sheila?"

So my mother finally agreed. "Well, you know best what you can do, Sheila, and if you want any help, or if things don't work out, then you can always have your bed here in the back room."

But finding a flat wasn't so easy. The difficulties arose not because of a shortage of accommodation, but mainly because I was blind. So many times we turned up for an appointment, and, as Anita told me afterwards, the face of the prospective landlord or landlady dropped when he or she realized I could not see. What kind of liability, I wonder, did they expect me to be? Would I blunder around and smash the furniture, overflow the bath and bring the plaster down, or simply cause the entire house to go up in flames? Those who did not mind me took exception to Emma or Tiss, or to both. It seemed hopeless.

Then, after nearly three months and countless disappointments, we finally found a small apartment. It was on Peel Street, in a large, rather decayed nineteenth-century country house. The three rooms smelled rather musty and were furnished with a few creaky chairs and tables. There was a kitchen converted from what may well have been a pantry in better days, and we were grateful for the sink and an oven, which Anita described to me as a genuine relic from the galley of the Ark.

Anita was the practical one of the household. As soon as we moved into the apartment she said, "We've got to be absolutely fair and straight down the line with expenses. I think we ought to have a kitty, particularly for the food. I'll get a can and you put three pounds in, and I'll do the same."

We were just deciding this important point when we had our first visitor. It was Graham, who had brought some cases of clothes for me. He did a tour of inspection and gave his verdict. "Not bad," he said, "not bad at all. But it needs a bit of brightening up. And you haven't got a clock."

"Yes, I have," I said. "It's in the bedroom."

"Oh, that. That's your braille alarm clock. I mean a clock that other people can see. Anita will want to tell the time too."

The following day Graham was back with a kitchen clock, which he screwed into the wall for us, as a housewarming gift. It was so characteristic of him to choose something that would link me with the sighted world.

There were other apartments in the house, and we were soon on speaking terms with our neighbors. But for a variety of reasons we never managed to hit it off with the fireman who lived immediately below us on the bottom floor. It was partly my fault. Anita used to go away a lot on weekends to stay with her parents and see her boyfriend in Hull, and she left me in charge. This made me nervous at first, but I soon got used to running the place on my own, with some help from Emma. It seemed an enormous step towards becoming more independent.

One of the first weekends that Anita was gone, before I had become used to the place, I decided to take the small kitchen waste basket down to the garbage cans outside. These were reached through the front garden and down a little ally, and they were arranged in a row next to the rock garden kept by the fireman. Emma came with me, although she was not in her harness, since we were not going on a proper outing. Somehow, a brick had been left in the middle of the alley. On harness, Emma would immediately have taken me around it. As it was, she merely stood by and watched. I tripped over the brick, and the rubbish flew all over the fireman, who had just emerged from his apartment, covering him with cigarette butts, banana skins and other assorted oddments.

Our relationship did not improve the following Saturday. Anita was once again away. I had decided that the kitchen needed a good cleanup, particularly the wastebasket that had figured so prominently in the previous week's episode. I boiled two kettles, filled the trash can with water and disinfectant, and left it for an hour below the sink. When I went to empty it, it felt ominously light. I put my hand in it.

No water. How was I to know that there had been a hole in the plastic? Or that the water had seeped through the floor and into the fireman's kitchen? Things were never the same again.

The most bizarre mistake I made occurred when we had been at the flat for a few months. In addition to Emma and Tiss, the animal population of the household had recently been increased by Anita's purchase of a pair of pet mice, called Ilk and Moke. I suppose they were sold as tame mice, although I would have sued the pet shop for false advertising. It was impossible to put a hand in their cage and bring it out unscratched. Tiss loathed them. When Anita was in Hull, I used to have to feed these small sharp-clawed monsters.

One weekend I had them in their cage on the kitchen table and had piled books on top of the cage so that Tiss could not leap onto their roof and stare and hiss down at them. On Sunday morning I got up and went with Emma into the kitchen to make a cup of tea. I knew I had left the matches on the table, and felt around for them. But then I heard something move near my hand. I almost had heart failure. I put out my hand for the box of matches, and there was the sound again: small claws. I was petrified. It had to be a mouse.

I went hot and cold. I thought I must have let one of them out when I was feeding them the previous day. What would Anita think? What if it escaped? Anita would assume Tiss had caught it. How could I get it back? I stood in my dressing gown trembling and then had a brainstorm. Much as I loathed the idea, I had to catch it, and I knew there was a can handy. I felt for this empty can and brought it up to the edge of the table. There I waited, quite still, for minutes on end.

Suddenly I heard a movement. Then, sure

enough, I felt the mouse—was it Ilk? Or was it Moke? I didn't care. Anyway, I felt him on the tin and quickly got him in and clapped my hand over the top, at the same time opening the cage. Before he could scratch or bite I had him back inside and crashed the cage door shut.

It took me several cups of tea to recover. But I could now face Anita on her return. When she did come back, late that evening, one of the first things she did was to inspect her mice. "Sheila," she cried, "my mice."

"Yes," I said haplessly, my heart turning over. Had I let them both out when I opened the cage?

"Sheila, what happened? There are three!"

"Three?"

"Yes, three—my white ones and a gray one."

Gray one! I immediately knew what had happened. I explained, and we collapsed with laughter. It occurred to me that it was quite the reverse of the Three Blind Mice!

Normally, however, things went smoothly, particularly when Anita was there. It was great fun to live with her, and I was well aware how lucky I was to have my own apartment, which is more than many sighted people have. We used to laugh a lot, and I was often amused by some of the Yorkshire expressions she came out with. One cold November day I had chosen a rather flimsy dress to wear.

"You can't wear that," Anita said.

"Why not?"

"You'll catch King Cough if you go out in that."

"King Cough? What's that?"

"Didn't your mother ever tell you? King Cough's three times worse than any other cough, and you catch your death of it."

Impressed by the idea and possible power of King Cough, I changed into something warmer. I imagine

that when I had first put the idea of sharing to A-
nita, she really must have thought there would be
some disadvantages in living with me, even though
she never said anything on the subject. I was that
much of a realist, at least. Yet for my part it was difficult to admit that I could not do everything a
sighted person could, and I was determined to show
that the handicap was not as bad as people thought.
In fact, I may possibly have surprised Anita by how
much I could do, even though I was blind. It meant
a great deal of hard work and concentration. Still, I
persevered.

I would do the vacuuming, while Anita dusted.
Sometimes, above the noise of the vacuum cleaner, I
would hear her laughing. I'd switch it off and say,
"Now what are you laughing at?" And she would
giggle, "Well, you've been over that bit of carpet
about six times—and there's a huge bit that still
needs doing only two inches away." So off I would go
again and wait for the next correction, until finally I
would have the entire carpet clean.

The food cupboard in the apartment was a source
of amusement after shopping expeditions. If I was in
charge I would buy only the food I wanted for the
next twenty-four hours, because too many cans and
packets were confusing. I would try to keep various
foodstuffs separate in the cupboard: a shelf for vegetables, part of another one for cans of fruit, a different part for cans of dog meat, and so on.

Sometimes my planning did not work out. Emma,
I think, very much enjoyed our best casserole steak
one night, and I did not pursue what happened to
the can of pet food she should have had. With packets and jars, one way of identifying the contents was
of course by smell. So if I wanted marmalade, I had
to take each jar out of the cabinet, unscrew the top
and sniff what was inside. With things like jams and

pickles this was fairly easy, if laborious; it also developed my sense of smell. But with salt or sugar I just had to wet my finger and taste—and sometimes got quite a surprise.

I was delving into the cabinet one evening when I suddenly decided that I really ought to do some entertaining. "Would you mind," I asked Anita, "if I invited friends over for a meal?"

"Mind? Of course I wouldn't mind. It's our home," she replied instantly.

I got in touch with my school friend Angela, whom I had not seen or heard of for some time. I knew she now had a boyfriend, and, as with so many of my friends, this was really the cause of my not seeing so much of her. As they say, two's company, but three's a crowd.

Angela was delighted to hear from me and sounded on top of the world when I asked her for dinner. Then I learned why. "I've got some news for you," she said.

"What's that?"

"I'm getting married next month."

"Oh. Congratulations. The same boyfriend, I hope."

She laughed. "Yes, John. You might have guessed. How about your boyfriends, Sheila?"

I automatically changed the subject. To me, it always seemed impossible for a blind person to mix with the opposite sex. I did not go to dances anymore; neither was Anita keen on night life, for her boyfriend was back in Hull. So I never met any boys through her. I was almost resigned to thinking that if blind people did get married, they were extremely lucky.

Angela agreed to come to the apartment the following Thursday. Anita asked, "Would you like me to cook, Sheila?"

"No, that's all right," I said. "She's my guest after all. I'll make a ham salad for her."

When Angela arrived, she was still bubbling over with plans for her marriage, and, once again, though I was very happy for her, I tried to get her to speak of something else. I attempted to recall some of the good times we had shared at school, but she did not seem receptive to this and carried on blithely about what a wonderful man John was.

Finally we all sat down to the table. I asked Angela to help herself, and although I could hear her transferring food from the salad bowl to her plate, she did not seem to take very long. "You haven't taken much, Angela."

There was a pause, and she cleared her throat in rather an embarrassed way. "Er—no. I haven't got a very big appetite."

Then she giggled nervously and said, "I suppose you do all the meals, Anita?"

I cut in immediately, "No, she certainly does not."

And Anita added quietly, "We share all the cooking and all the housework."

"Oh," said Angela, "I'm sorry, Sheila, but I didn't know you could cook."

"Well, whether you have sight or not," I explained, "a lot of cooking is actually done by touch. If you're boiling potatoes, you put a fork in them to test if they're cooked through. If you're roasting a piece of meat, you put a skewer in it from time to time. I know that people who can see don't rely on this entirely, but for me it's really important, and you'd be surprised at what I can do. . . ."

"But I don't understand how you manage to use the oven," said Angela.

"Ah," I said, "I'll let you in on a little secret: the regulator knob that controls the temperature. We've had a braille regulator fitted to our terrible old

oven, and I can feel the right setting for whatever I
want to bake or roast. The only thing I don't do
much is frying. The fat spits—and you can imagine
what would happen if I put a skewer in a fried egg
to test it!"

We all laughed, and it seemed to relieve the tension that had built up in Angela's presence. But a
moment later, she put her foot in it again. She said
to Anita, "What's it like living with a big dog
around the place, Anita?"

Anita replied, rather sharply I thought, "Emma's
not a dog. She's part of the family." And I heard
Emma stir from underneath the table to confirm this
central fact of our existence together.

After that, the occasion went limp. Angela had obviously changed a great deal. She had forgotten what
I was like to be with, and our tennis days. I was,
truth to tell, quite relieved when she decided it was
time to leave.

"She didn't eat much," I remarked to Anita afterwards, as we cleared the table.

"No," said Anita a little grimly. "I could have
killed her. She must be used to having her meals all
dished up like pictures from a *Good Housekeeping*
recipe book, because she looked at your tomatoes
and lettuce in the bowl as if they were something
Tiss had dragged in."

"Oh, that was it," I said. "Well, at least you don't
mind my heaping everything into the salad bowl and
not arranging it."

"No. It all goes down the same way, and it all
tastes the same, fancy arrangement or not." We
laughed about this, but I did not invite Angela
again.

There was one thing I could *not* manage on my
own, and for which I had to rely a great deal on A-

nita. That was dress sense. It is very difficult to pick
the right clothes if you can't see the color and can
only touch the garments to get an idea of the
material and style. When I went into a shop in the
days before I lived with Anita, it was very often a
case of Never-mind-the-quality, feel-the-width. But
with her advice I could wear clothes that I knew
were fashionable.

She would come along with me to the shops, or, if
I went with Emma, I would take the outfit home on
approval, try it on, and ask Anita's opinion. "No, it's
just not you," she might say, or, "No, I don't think
so. It makes you look about ninety." So back to the
shop the outfit would go. I suppose I was really
wearing clothes that Anita herself liked, rather than
those that I might like if I could have seen them,
but I still found it very liberating. Anita, after all,
was my age and kept up with the fashion magazines,
and for the first time in my life, I felt I too was part
of the fashion scene.

As well as helping with my clothes, Anita was also
able to tell me if my hair looked right. She was my
mirror. But the best thing about her was that she
treated me as a paid-up member of the human race.
She had a great sense of honesty and never made embarrassing allowances for the fact that I could not
see.

There was, however, one time I had to be wary of
being with her, and that was when we would do our
shopping together. It was pleasant for Emma to have
Anita take over guiding me. Emma did not have her
harness on, and she could go on a lead like any other
dog out for a walk. But it was not always so good for
me, because I would occasionally trip or collide painfully with a pole, and Anita would say, "Oh, Sheila,
I'm so sorry. I was looking in a store window, I

didn't see that." In the end, I am afraid, I went back to relying entirely on Emma, even when we all went out together.

It was while I was at the flat that I came to realize how close a bond had grown between Emma and me—and not only on my side. When I first had Emma, she was never less than splendid in her work, despite her independence in choosing her own routes. Yet I got the impression that, although I needed Emma, she did not really need me. She would look after me when we were going along the street, but indoors at the house where we first lived she would never bark when there was a knock on the door. She had no protective instinct towards me.

Once we had settled in at the apartment, Emma's attitude gradually changed. We began to spend a great deal of time on our own, and of course she was with me twenty-four hours a day. She would follow me about, which she had not done before, and would never let me out of her sight—even in the bathroom. Not only did we begin to walk with the same pace and kind of step, but we seemed to develop an instinct for knowing one another's thoughts.

One incident really convinced me of our uncanny telepathy. I used to do the shopping for the weekend at lunchtime on Fridays in a little area called Netherfield. Emma always knew it was Friday, and I never had to say anything to her; she would simply take me to Netherfield, whereas on every other day we went for our usual walk. One Monday, however, I wanted to take my watch to be repaired, and the nearest jeweler was in Netherfield. I had never been to this jeweler's before, and as I did not know where it was exactly, I got full directions from a friend.

I assumed Emma would think we were going for our usual outing, and for some reason I did not tell her that the plan had changed. We went out of the office to the main road. But instead of proceeding on our Monday route, Emma unhesitatingly headed for the shopping center at Netherfield, entered a store, and sat down.

I was astounded. We were in the jeweler's. How could she possibly have known we were going to our Friday area on a Monday? Even more astonishing, how could she possibly have known we were going to that shop? I certainly hadn't said a word to her about it.

"How did you *know*, Emma?" I asked. And I could hear her tail beating on the floor. "Oh, all right," I said, "I give in. I'll never try to keep you in the dark again." And I never did.

6

DON

While we were at the apartment, our local radio station, Radio Nottingham, came on the air for the first time. One of the programs introduced, *Wednesday Club*, was especially for blind people. It was run by George Miller, who was a newspaper reporter and blind himself. It always astonished me that someone who could not see was able to do this kind of work. Yet he not only made his living from journalism; he did the job magnificently.

One day, George got in touch with me to ask if I would go on the program to talk about guide-dogs. I said I would, but I did not very much like the idea of sitting in front of a microphone and reciting a lot of facts and figures about guide-dogs, because I didn't think the audience could be held like that. A better way of getting across just what the dogs did would be to have some sort of practical demonstration involving Emma and me. So I suggested having a bet that we could get from any one part of Nottingham to another faster than a sighted person.

George laughed and said they would think about it. A day later he rang back and agreed to my idea, and told me that Tony Church, the producer, would be the one with whom I would have the contest. He made it quite clear, however, that everyone at Radio Nottingham thought I was out of my mind, and that Emma and I had as much chance of winning as a three-legged horse in a race.

Tony mapped out a route and told me he would disclose it on the day of the taping. Emma and I accordingly turned up outside the Radio Nottingham studios. Tony was there to meet us, with his tape recorder and microphone.

"Well, this is the famous Emma, the dog that's going to beat me, is it?"

"Yes, it is," I said, while I imagined Emma giving him a piercing look of confirmation that this was indeed what was going to happen.

"All right," said Tony. "Do you know Trinity Square?"

Trinity Square? This was great. "Yes," I answered. "Very well."

"Well, now, where in Trinity Square would you like to head for?"

I thought for a moment and then decided. "The forty-nine bus stop."

"Fine," said Tony, and off we went. We had to cross quite a few busy main roads in order to reach this particular square. At first I could hear Tony behind me, using his tape recorder to give a commentary on what was going on, but before long his voice was drowned out by the noise of the traffic.

Emma and I pounded on, Emma seeming more agile and nimble than ever. At last we reached Trinity Square, and the bus station post. Tony did not arrive until a few minutes later. Rather out of breath and somewhat stunned, he said, "Congratulations, and apologies. You were right and we were wrong."

It was not until I heard the tape played back in the studio that I learned what had happened. It was no doubt entertaining for the listeners, but it also enlightened me about the way Emma worked. She had taken me around many obstacles about which I was completely unaware. She had also led me across a pedestrian crossing. Emma had sat down at the crossing, and we had waited until I could hear the traffic stop. I remember at this point that Emma got up first and crossed the road. What I did not know was that a bus had pulled up at the crossing, and the driver had leaned out of his cab and waved Emma over. As we reached the other side, Tony had come panting up to the crossing. But the bus moved on at that moment and left him stranded. He then ran along that side of the road, trying to keep up. When he did finally cross and catch up with us, he trod on Emma's tail, which made her move even faster. Then, when he attempted to cross the next road, the same sort of thing happened again. The traffic waited for us, but not for Tony. As we reached Trinity Square, we were well in front, and Emma, according to the tape, had time to stop and look in a shop window that seemed to interest her. It had a huge notice: SALE ON.

That program for Radio Nottingham was the genesis of my friendship with George Miller. He was extremely likable, full of vivacity and zest for life.

From then on he often used to phone me to discuss the *Wednesday Club* programs. He was committed to helping other blind people, and rightly considered the whole venture a worthwhile contribution in this direction. Sometimes he called and chatted about a piece of news concerning the blind, or he consulted me about guide-dog work.

One evening, George said he had a friend with him, someone named Don Hocken. He asked if I would like a word with Don. Don was in the same room and could hear the conversation through the speaker that had been fitted onto George's telephone to leave his hands free for his braille machine. He came on the line and chatted, and if it is possible to fall in love immediately over the telephone, I certainly did.

When Don told me he was a podiatrist, I'm afraid I laughed. I imagined someone condemned to a fate of cutting other people's toenails. He set me straight, however. It was, he said, more complicated than that. But he did not seem to mind my laughter one bit, although I later learned how much his work meant to him and what a close interest he took in his patients.

Don was fond of dogs and had heard from George about Emma, so we talked for some time about her, and poor George hardly got a word in at all. When we hung up I could not get over the sound of Don's soft, deep voice, and the conversation kept replaying itself in my mind. I discovered afterwards that Don had first met George as a patient. On the day of the first consultation, not realizing George was blind, Don had put his groping approach to the office door down to excess alcohol! They struck up a friendship, and George had been helping Don with some of his own writing efforts.

A few evenings later George called again, and Don

was there too. I was thrilled. When he came on the line I wondered what he looked like, but, strangely, I felt on a par with him in a way that would have been impossible if we had been introduced face to face. He told me that he had been invited to the open house the following Saturday at Radio Nottingham, and suddenly I felt nervous. I had also been invited, and I wondered whether I dared go. I simply did not want to face the fact that if he had illusions they might dissolve when he saw me. Moreover, I never believed that a sighted man could really be attracted to a woman who was blind. But I thought it over, and in the end my curiosity won: I decided I would go.

I remember that day in August 1968 so well. I went through my entire wardrobe wondering what to wear. I finally settled on my best green dress and newest shoes. I had been to the hairdresser, and I kept asking Anita, "Do I look all right? Is my hair okay? Do I really look presentable? What do you honestly think?" Anita kept reassuring me, "Oh, Sheila, you look fine, you really do. Don't be silly."

But it was impossible for me to compare myself accurately with other people and therefore judge for myself what I looked like. As a result, I always felt that I could not be as well-dressed as anyone else or that my hair could look as good as theirs. When people said, "You look nice," I could never be sure that they were not making allowances for the fact that I was blind.

At last, after these great preparations, Emma and I set off. Emma knew I was excited, because she pushed herself forward in her harness and wagged her tail. I told her all about Don. "He sounds very nice, Emma," I said, "but I don't know what he'll make of us, I really don't." Emma continued wagging her tail, but the further we went, the more nervous I became. Silly, but there it was. I could not understand it at the time, but this meeting seemed so very, very important and special.

We arrived at Radio Nottingham, and, once inside, I could hear a big crowd. Eventually I managed to get someone to find George for me. We sat talking in a corner, and then I heard this unmistakable voice some distance away. I thought, *I wonder if he's seen me? I wonder what he thinks? Perhaps he's seen me and doesn't want to come over and meet us after all.*

When he moved closer I could make out what he was saying. Don was talking to a girl with a young, attractive voice, and he said, "The last time I saw you, you were in bed." I was astonished and thought, *Well, would you believe it? He's just one of these characters who sweep girls off their feet and straight into bed.* I felt terribly let down. Then I heard more of the conversation. It turned out that while Don had been visiting his mother in the hospital, this girl had been in the next bed!

At last he said good-bye to her. I heard the approach of footsteps, and the same voice, much nearer, said, "Hello, Sheila." In the same instant I knew he was smiling. Emma got up and gave him a huge welcome. He patted her and made a great fuss of her, but he quickly turned his attention to me.

We sat down and began talking, and it was as if we had known each other for years. He described the studio in detail to me—the control panels, the double windows and everything about the surroundings and the people who were there. But it was not only the description that was marvelous, but the fact that Don knew I was cut off and had immediately done what he could to tell me all about what was going on.

"Would you like to tour the studio with me?" he asked eventually. I said I would and was surprised and delighted when he didn't immediately clutch at my arm and try to drag me around. Instead, he offered his arm for me to put my hand on, which is the best and easiest way to guide a blind person. He was not a bit embarrassed, and when we got to the control panel he insisted on my feeling all the dials and buttons. "This is the control panel, Sheila. Feel the control here. This is the window that looks out over the studio . . ." Don seemed to have an instinctive grasp of how to make things come alive to someone who is blind. I felt completely relaxed and happy with him.

Later on in the afternoon he suggested to George that we all go to have some tea together. At first I did not much like the idea, as I did not want Don to see my difficulties when everything was so wonderful. I tried to make excuses, but he would not listen.

"Come on," he said, "I know a really nice place just up the road." Finally he persuaded me, and Emma and I walked in front of George, who was being guided by Don. He had told me exactly where the restaurant was, and we arrived a little in front of them. I was pleased, because I wanted to show that with Emma's guidance I was well able to cope.

We got permission for Emma to come in (always a problem in restaurants, and not one that the magic word "guide-dog" would necessarily solve). Once inside, she curled up under the table, and Don once again thoughtfully described the surroundings. We ordered steak, and Don offered to cut it up for me. As always I refused and later paid for this small show of independence. The second time I got my fork to my mouth with nothing on it, I heard Don laugh and say, "You've missed again." I was so humiliated that I blushed from my toes to the roots of my hair. I wanted him to accept me as a normal person. Yet his laughter had no unkindness in it, and

somehow his laughing it off in this way did make
things easier in the end.

After the meal, Don drove Emma and me back to
Peel Street. As we said good-bye outside the apartment, just before he got back into the car, he handed
me something. I felt it. It was a rose, which I supposed he had taken out of his buttonhole. When I
got in, I put the flower in a vase and cherished it. I
never wanted to throw it away and kept it long after
the bloom had gone.

In the days that followed I kept going over in my
mind the details of that Saturday. I had an uneasy
feeling that I would never hear from Don again—
that it had been a lovely day, and that was it. I pictured him as tall and fair and moustached. I knew
he was tall because his voice came from above me,
and I knew he was quite broad-shouldered from taking his arm on the tour of the studio. I was quite
glad that Anita had not been there and that there
was no one to give me a description of Don, because
I always preferred the way I imagined people to be.

A few days went by, and I was beginning to think
my fears about his not getting in touch again were
right, when a voice I instantly recognized came over
the switchboard. I knew Don would not be phoning
to order our latest model sewage pump. He wanted
to take me out that evening. That evening! I was so
excited that for the rest of the afternoon there was a
high percentage of calls to wrong extensions all over
the office.

On the way home I told Emma about it. By that
time, I had mentioned Don's name to her so often
that she was quite familiar with it, and she wagged
her tail in reply. Anita was still at work, so there was
only Emma to share my excitement. I remember
feeling the warmth of the sun in my bedroom as I
started to change and thinking how the world sud-

denly seemed to have become a warm and marvelous place.

That summer evening seemed more scented than any I could remember. As we went out I said to myself, *Someone wants to see me, really wants to see me.* My shoes hardly seemed to touch the pavement as Emma took me to meet Don, and at the same time I thought, *If it were not for Emma, none of this would be possible.*

Don had said he would pick us up at a point on Mansfield Road, for a reason which brought the only cloud of the evening—and the only cloud surrounding our whole relationship. Don was still married, and it was difficult to choose a time and place to meet. Friends had already told me that he and his wife no longer got on together, that the marriage did not work. And, in the way friends have of giving gratuitous advice, they said I was foolish to become involved with a married man.

Yet they also told me that Don was not the kind of man who would have casual affairs, so I knew that in order to ask me out, he must have thought seriously about the implications, and he must also have thought a great deal of me. For my part, I had no wish to encourage anyone to leave his wife. I felt strongly about this, and it was only because of what I learned about Don and the state of his marriage from my friends that my conscience was eased.

He took me that first evening to a little pub called The Three Wheatsheaves on the outskirts of Nottingham. I can remember few of the details, except everything seemed magical. The pub had a cozy, welcoming smell and atmosphere. Emma sat under the table again as we talked, and at one point Don tentatively took my hand. He was fifteen years older than I and had a tremendous gift of making me feel

I was the one person of importance in the entire universe.

It seemed that we had been in the pub only a few minutes (although we must have been there for almost two hours) before the owner began to close up. He had an extraordinarily deep voice. In fact, whenever we went to his pub after that we never said, "Let's go to The Three Wheatsheaves." We called it The Gruff Man's Voice, and it became our own name for the very special place where we spent our first evening together.

In the days that followed, I knew I was in love with Don. But did he love me? Somehow I thought it slightly unfair of me to expect such a thing. Yet Don never gave a hint that my being unable to see was of any importance. His complete acceptance, in fact, provided my greatest encouragement to get on and be like everyone else and to cover the frustrations of being blind. When someone said to me, "It must be nice for you going out with Don. He must be a great help to you," I therefore became rather irritated. I hated the idea that a sighted person was a sort of spare limb to do things for me. Whatever else happened, I wanted to keep my independence.

But the doubts remained. Don could see. I was blind. Therefore he could not possibly be in love with me. The logic seemed inescapable. At the same time I was certain, yet skeptical, of my own love for him. Love was something I had read about in braille paperbacks, and invariably concerned sighted people. How could it happen to me?

One evening Don called and said that the car had broken down, and he would not be able to meet me. I hardly heard him say, "I've phoned the garage, and they're coming along, and I'll call you if they can fix it." All I thought was, *This is it. He's decided he doesn't want to see me anymore. This is the excuse;*

he doesn't want to be involved with someone who's blind.

"Yes," I said, "all right." I put the phone down and paced up and down the apartment, willing myself not to cry. Emma came up to me and rested her nose on my knee. We sat like that for hours. *She understands,* I thought.

The phone rang, and my heart turned over. It was Don again. "I'm sorry, Sheila. They've had a look at it, and the alternator's gone; they can't get a new one until tomorrow. I am sorry . . ." It was just as well that Anita happened to be away. I did not want to talk to anyone. I did not go to bed, but simply sat in a waking nightmare.

The next day I went about my work like an automaton, until I took an incoming call at about ten o'clock and heard Don's familiar voice. As if nothing had happened, he said the car had been fixed, and he asked to meet me that evening instead. How could he have known what I had been through, or that my anxieties, rooted in and fostered by my blindness, were all too quick to flourish? From then on I never doubted how much I loved Don.

About a week later we were sitting in Don's car with the rain pouring down outside—somehow that made us feel more together. Don suddenly turned to me and said, "It won't always be like this, you know."

I didn't know what to say. I think I made some noncommittal remark, yet I knew the situation was changing, melting into something else.

Don went on, "Will you wait till I'm free?"

I felt like opening the car door then and there and getting out to do a dance with Emma on the pavement despite the pouring, freezing, December rain.

Would I wait? Of course I would!

"Well, it won't be easy," said Don. And then he told me why. His daughter, Susan, was then only nine. He felt he had a responsibility to her not to leave until she was older and could understand what was happening.

"How old," I asked, "do you think she must be before you can tell her?"

"About fourteen."

Fourteen. That meant five years before we could be together. Five years seemed an eternity to me, since I was only twenty-one myself.

But I could not be gloomy at the thought. At last I knew he really loved me, and I, in turn, loved him so much that I would wait until the end of time if need be.

7

INDEPENDENCE

So my life became centered around Don: snatching meetings whenever possible and experiencing a terrible emptiness whenever we were apart. There was a lot of waiting for him, because he invariably did not finish at the clinic until about nine in the evening and very often was kept even later by patients. Sometimes, if it had started to rain, Emma and I would be soaked by the time he arrived. Don once told me that it was seeing us both standing there waiting, looking like orphans—me with my hat wet and Emma with her tail down and coat dark—that made him realize how much I cared for him.

At about this time I began to feel that my working life was in need of a change. The long journey back and forth to Industrial Pumps was beginning to pall. It took Emma and me the best part of an hour. So when a new management took over, I decided to start looking for another job. If I had known then what frustration and misery this would entail, I suppose I might never have made the decision.

Before then I had never fully realized how terribly handicapped a blind man or woman is. The main difficulty, which began to become an obsession, was that others would not accept me. Don accepted me without question, and so did Anita; yet their enlightened attitudes had possibly cushioned me against the indifference and outright rejection of so many of the rest of the human race.

I had nearly eight years' experience working a busy switchboard and was as efficient as any telephone operator. But despite this, I was not good enough, apparently, for most employers. I used to take the newspaper home every night, and when Anita was there, she read down the want ads for me, while I made a note in braille of the numbers. When I called the firms listed, the dialogue went along these lines:

"I'm inquiring about the vacancy you've advertised for a telephone operator."

"Ah yes, could you give us some details of your experience?"

I would then tell them about my job, and that I was used to working a PABX Number Two switchboard.

"Good, that sounds fine."

Then I would drop the bombshell: "There's something else I must tell you. I'm a blind person, but that doesn't make any difference in my ability to operate the switchboard, and I have a guide-dog."

I needn't have bothered. I could almost hear the waning of interest over the phone, like a balloon deflating.

"Yes, well, thank you for calling. We'll keep you in mind, but we have had quite a few applicants already."

This, at least, was some attempt to cushion the blow. But from time to time, the reception was brutally insensitive: "Oh, I'm sorry, we couldn't possibly consider employing anyone who's blind. The office you'd have to work in is upstairs."

"But my dog and I go up and down stairs every day of our lives."

"I'm sorry, we couldn't possibly consider you. I'm afraid you'd be too much of a risk."

When I tried to argue the point with the boss of one firm, he actually hung up on me.

Worst of all, perhaps, was the way that vacancies magically became filled as soon as I mentioned that I was blind. The utter dishonesty and hypocrisy made me want to scream. Eventually I decided that there was only one way around the problem. If I was to be considered ineligible just because I was blind, I simply would not mention the fact. I would give my qualifications, and if asked to go for an interview, I would confront my prospective employers. After several months I was desperate, but I had nothing to lose.

Immediately I had two firms interested in me, and both wanted to interview me on the same day. At the first place I went to, a lace-manufacturing company, I sensed surprise when I turned up with a guide-dog. But Emma settled down at once and curled up beside me as I sat opposite the man asking the questions. Everything went off without a hitch. The office manager was then called in and took me down to where the switchboard was. I felt to see if it

Sheila aged five

Sunday School Whitsuntide Walk

Emma at three weeks—back row, second from right

(Yorkshire Post)

Emma at eight weeks

Leamington Spa—trainer Brian Peel on left

(Walter Watson)

Paddy Wansborough with Emma, Sarah and Miranda

At Work

*(Nottingham
Evening Post)*

Sponsored walk
through Nottingham

*(Nottingham
Evening Post)*

Sheila, Don and Emma on holiday in Cornwall, 1973

Ming and Ohpas   (*Langland Ross*)

Emma and Ming

(*Oliver Hatch*)

Emma now

(Oliver Hatch)

Emma—retired   *(Oliver Hatch)*

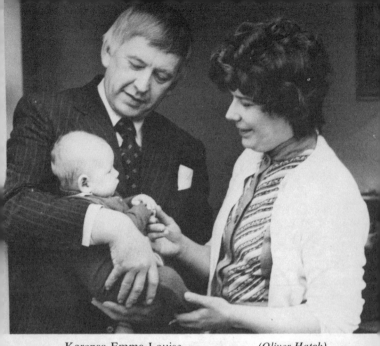

Kerensa Emma Louise   *(Oliver Hatch)*

was the same type that I was used to, and it was. "But," he said, "how do you operate it? It's not adapted for a blind person." So I explained that the Post Office converted them free, and the job was offered to me on the spot.

It was an incredible feeling to be able to go to the second interview knowing that whatever happened I would be taking a new job. The next vacancy was at Whytecliffe's, a big garage not far from the middle of Nottingham. Once again they were surprised at Emma, but having been presented on their doorstep with the prospect of a blind employee, they made no bones about going through the usual procedure. Emma again curled up quietly, this time under my chair. But although she just lay there, she played an important part in the interview. It turned out that the personnel manager who asked me the questions was a breeder of Springer spaniels. His inquiries concerned Emma almost as much as my expertise with a switchboard, and I quickly got the impression that he had become besotted at first sight with the chocolate-colored creature under my chair. I told him all the things that Emma did for me, and I am sure she was a deciding factor. I was offered the job, and I took it in preference to the other partly because the money was better, and also because Whytecliffe's was only a fifteen-minute walk from the flat.

By the time I started the new job the Post Office engineers had already converted the switchboard. The other girls in the office were surprised when I arrived on the first morning with a big Labrador. Most of them realized that Emma was a guide-dog, but one girl came up to me and said, "How is it you can bring your dog to work? It's not fair. I'd like to bring mine." She was taken aback when I explained why Emma was there.

One or two of the girls began to doubt that I was really blind at all. They had looked out of the office windows and watched Emma and me crossing the street and coming straight to the door of the office. They could not believe that it was Emma who was responsible. In addition, Emma was so good at taking me anywhere I wanted to go inside the office that I soon learned how to get about on my own. Despite the fact that they had seen me operating the switchboard by touch, taking messages in braille and feeling my notebook for numbers, they began to think there was some catch. They thought that somehow—for what reason I have never fathomed—I was perpetrating an enormous hoax.

So they decided they would settle the matter. I worked at the far end of a long office that had desks on either side and a narrow passageway in between. At the opposite end was the cafeteria. After Emma had brought me there for the first few days at coffee break, I didn't bother to put her on harness for the walk. Emma came too, but she always raced well ahead of me, because she knew there would be a bowl of milk waiting for her.

What happened on the morning the girls decided to find out about my blindness may sound mean, even cruel; it was certainly thoughtless, but I am sure it arose from quite genuine, though stupid, suspicions. They left several chairs and other objects in my way, so when it was time for the break, Emma charged off in front of me, and I immediately crashed from obstacle to obstacle. I finally knocked over a stepladder. There was a silence of deep embarrassment. One girl later came and said she was sorry, but that they really did think I could see. My own reaction, once I had gotten over the whole business, was of even greater pride in Emma, that she could convince them that I was not blind at all.

Since we lived on Peel Street and worked at Whytecliffe's, Emma became very familiar with the center of Nottingham. She learned the names of all the stores and bus stations I used. We did a lot of shopping at the big Co-op in Parliament Street. I only had to put her harness on and say, "Find the Co-op, Emma," and off we would go, her tail wagging furiously.

Emma adored shopping. One of the reasons she liked it so much was that she made the rules. Rule One was that we could go anywhere we liked, anywhere at all, but the first place visited had to be a pet shop. Wherever we went, the route had to be planned to take in one of these vital stores. We would go in, buy bone-shaped biscuits, chews, vitamin chocolate drops or a rubber toy, and after that the rest of the operation could proceed.

Rule Two about shopping was that we must never—whatever else was happening, and no matter how many of them lay along the route—miss an opportunity of visiting a butcher's shop. It was a terrible weakness of Emma's, and we became known in every butcher's within a five-mile radius of the middle of Nottingham. We would be going along, and I might, as well as concentrating on Emma, be thinking about what Anita and I were going to have for supper, when suddenly with no warning, I would find myself in a shop with sawdust under my feet, an unmistakable smell, and no intention of buying so much as an ounce of meat. It was very embarrassing. But the butchers took it all in good spirit and got to know Emma so well that occasionally she got a bone for her initiative—and, of course, for her good looks.

Yet once seriously down to the business of shopping, Emma was quite amazing. Her mind was an encyclopedia of stores' names. I would have only to say the word and we were there. She was equally astonishing, if not more so, in a big store like the Co-op. She knew not only how to get there but also the location of every department and counter. If I said, "Find the shoe department," I'd be taken there instantly, with never a mistake.

One evening in the spring of 1969 Anita came home and seemed very subdued. "Sheila," she said, "I've got something to tell you. The office is going to move me to Grantham."

"Oh," I said. "When?"

"Not until July, but I feel dreadful because I know you can't afford to keep the apartment by yourself." This was true. I earned nine pounds a week at the time, and the rent we shared was six pounds a week. The whole thing came as a shock, and it was not really the financial aspect that was upsetting. I felt so terribly sad at the prospect of breaking up our happy partnership.

Of course, what I longed to do more than anything else was to marry Don. But meanwhile, the idea of living alone filled me with misgivings. It was, of course, the ultimate step towards genuine independence, but it also meant I really had to be able to fend for myself. I had no fears of being lonely because Emma was there, and with her help I felt quite capable of coping. But there would be no one to read my letters for me and no one to tell me the instructions on a packet of instant soup or cake mix. What would I do if a fuse went? The light did not matter, but the use of an iron or toaster did. On the plus side, I would be able to plan the apartment so that I would know exactly where everything was, and no one would make even the slightest alteration to things as I had left them. (This was something visitors occasionally did that drove me into a frenzy; even if it was only an ashtray they had moved, I occasionally had to spend half an hour feeling all over for it.)

There was nothing to do but to begin looking for somewhere else to live, and at least there was a bit of time in which to do it. Luckily, I had been for a while on the local housing project list, but there was nothing available. However, the people who ran the project were very pleasant and noted my circumstances. The weeks ticked by. There was nothing I could afford in the local papers or through the rental agents, so I went to the project again. This time they said they would do what they could as quickly as possible. I think I probably owe the result more to Emma sitting in the office looking pathetic than to my own powers of persuasion: The man who interviewed me on this occasion made a great fuss of her, and she responded in her most appealing way. Within a week I had a letter offering me an apartment in a block on the Ilkeston Road, about four miles from where we were living at the time.

I was greatly relieved, but then came the bad news. Animals were not allowed in the project, and though an exception could be made because Emma was a guide-dog, I would have to part with Tiss. He and Emma had become very attached to each other. Tiss would always wait for us in the evening, sitting on the gate of the Peel Street house, and often spent the night sleeping on top of Emma. I wondered what the best course was and then decided to put an advertisement in the paper. After a day or two I received a phone call from a family in Beeston. I questioned them very closely about their background, because I was determined that Tiss go to a good home. They seemed the right sort of people and I heard from them later that Tiss had settled down and seemed quite happy.

When the apartment in the project at last fell vacant, my mother came along to help clean it up. This first encounter with my new home was gloomy. It seemed all the apartments were the same, each one a little box on what I imagined to be a never-ending series of identical floors. It took my mother ages to find Number 103, the apartment I had been allotted, and when at last we got in and put our luggage and cleaning gear down, she said, "Sheila, this is terrible. I'm so worried. You'll never find your way in and out. Whatever possessed the rental office to give a blind person an apartment on the fifth floor?"

"But, Mom," I said, "I've got Emma. I don't need a special place because I can't see. I just don't want that sort of thing."

But she persisted. "No, I'm going to get it changed tomorrow."

I pleaded with her. "No, Mom, don't. It's perfectly all right. Emma's quite capable of taking me in and out."

I finally persuaded her, and when we had cleaned the flat more or less to my mother's satisfaction, we stopped for tea. I hadn't brought any with me, so one of us had to go out to the grocer's. My mother immediately said, "I'll go."

"No, no," I said, "I'll go with Emma. We'll make a start on getting to know the area."

She was horrified. "No, Sheila, I'm not letting you go down there on your own."

So, back to the old argument. "But, Mom, I won't *be* on my own. I've got Emma. We've got to start sometime, and it might just as well be now."

I knew that Emma, in fact, was probably more capable than my mother and I put together, but I did not say so. To be fair, my mother had not seen Emma's skill at working in a new area, because she had brought me to the new apartment and Emma had been off duty. It might almost have been better, and quicker, if I had relied on Emma to begin with. Anyway, my mother gave in, and we set off along the open-sided landing.

Emma had no difficulty finding the elevator and we got off at the ground floor. But since I did not know the surroundings at all, I could not follow my usual procedure of asking Emma to find a particular store. Instead, I had to ask her to locate a shop, any shop, where I could ask for directions. I said to her as we went along, "Emma, we're going to buy some tea, sugar and milk." Whether by fluke, or because Emma actually recognized its appearance I shall never know, but the very first place we tried was a corner grocery store.

When we got back I could tell that my mother was surprised, and then I realized she was still not convinced about Emma's ability. "Oh, back already," she said. "Couldn't you find the elevator?"

"Of course we did. Look, I've got all the groceries."

"Well, how did you get back so quickly? Did someone bring you?"

"No, Emma brought me back."

"I don't believe it. She couldn't have found her way so quickly around here."

"Well, she did."

Then my mother had an inspiration. "I know," she said. "That dog can read the numbers on the doors."

After my mother left, I went out to call Don. My mother had told me where she had seen a phone booth. It was just across the main road outside the flats. Emma knew the words "phone booth" and she took me straight across the road to the one I wanted. But when I got inside and felt for the receiver, it was missing. The booth had obviously been vandalized. I felt terribly frustrated and, worse, had no idea what to do. I was desperate to phone Don and tell him how the move had gone and what the new apartment was like. I said to Emma, "There's no phone. What are we going to do?"

I finally decided we had better search around and hope that someone would come by who could tell us where another pay phone was. I told Emma to go down the road, but she did not respond. Instead she took me back across the main road, and I imagined she thought I had made my call and we were heading back to the flat. "No, Emma," I said, "I haven't made my call. We've got to find another phone." So on we went, but then she took me down a strange side road that had bricks and bits of rubble on it. I learned later that both demolition and construction were going on here at the same time. I tried to get Emma to stop, but she went on relentlessly, across the uneven ground until she turned left into another road and sat down.

I sensed that there was something there, put my hand out and felt the ridged metal ribs and glass of a phone booth. How Emma had managed to get us there has remained an unsolved mystery. Neither of us had ever been along that road before in our lives!

8

EVENING CLASSES

One day soon after the move I received a phone call from Kath Hill. Kath was a guide-dog owner with whom I had been put in touch by my home teacher at the time I was applying for Emma. I had never met her, although we chatted now and then on the telephone.

"Sheila," she asked, "what do you think about beginning evening classes especially for the blind?"

Since my Writer's Craft activities with Anita, I had not been to any classes. "It sounds like a great idea," I said, "but what kind of classes?"

"Makeup and beauty," she replied. "I've had a call from someone who wants to start a class for blind people on this sort of thing, provided there's sufficient support. Do you think enough people would be interested?"

"Well," I said, "I most certainly would be. I'm sure lots of others would as well."

The more we discussed it, the more attractive the idea became. I had always worn some makeup but never been able to do anything elaborate. I used foundation cream and lipstick—foundation cream was easy to put on because it went all over the face, and lipstick, too, was quite simple because I was able to feel my lips. I thought it would be nice to learn to use other beauty aids.

So the course was arranged by the local board of

education, and, in particular, by David Selby, who at the time was head of the adult education activities. He was a very forward-looking man, someone who thought beyond the confines of the subjects normally taught at evening classes, and he had a particular interest in helping the blind.

The numbers had to be limited, of course, so that the teacher could cope. I called all my blind friends and received a good response. One of the major problems—how to get to the classes—was solved in advance. The Nottingham Blind Institution agreed to make a minibus and driver available to us.

The first evening brought great excitement. About ten of us had enrolled, including six with guide-dogs. As we joined the minibus, much greeting and tail-wagging went on, particularly between Emma and Kath's dog, Rachel.

Our teacher was Joan Dickson, and in spite of the fact that she had no experience with the blind, she was very encouraging. That first evening she dealt with basic skin care. She told each of us what skin type we had and what color hair. Then she explained which color eyes usually went with which kind of hair, and how the foundation cream to be used was determined.

She also told us about face packs, something blind people would normally never think of using. But the best part of the course came later, when we had to use various kinds of makeup we had never before thought possible: eye shadow, mascara and eye liner. I had no idea how to apply them. Joan started by telling us, "First of all, you have to match your colors. If you're going to wear a green dress, then you want a green eye shadow." It may sound odd, but that had never occurred to me, and it was a minor revelation. "Then," she went on, "you have to match your lipstick to your eye shadow and dress. In the case of a green dress and eye shadow you could use a pink shade of lipstick." I was fascinated.

But one problem still remained: How actually to apply the eye shadow. Joan came round to each of us and demonstrated, and we learned by feeling. When she put the eye shadow on me, I realized it could be done by touch. The bone above the eye and at the side is a good guide, while the eyelash could be felt as a limiting landmark for shadow. Mascara was a little more difficult, and even with practice we succeeded only partially. No one found it possible to put mascara on the lower lashes. Eye liner was easier because the line of the top of the lashes could be felt and followed. But although I say it was easier, it all took a lot of practice and care before we got it right, and Joan was endlessly patient in coming around and telling us how we were getting on. Fairly frequently we had to take off whatever we had put on and start all over again.

Nail polish was another beauty aid Joan dealt with. I had used it before, but by the technique of covering my nails and the surrounding skin. When it was dry, I would peel off the polish from the skin. A girl at work had once watched me doing this and observed, "You're getting polish all over the skin around your nails. I'd always thought how beautifully you put it on." I replied, "Well, now you know how I do it." But Joan helped me to apply the polish correctly and efficiently by touching the outside of the nail first, over the cuticle, then brushing upwards to the top.

The class was a huge success. When I went out with Don, I could at last make myself up properly. People we met sometimes asked, "Who put your makeup on for you?" I was now able to answer, "I did," and it gave me a terrific feeling of completeness, and of being equal to everyone else.

The makeup and beauty classes went so well, in fact, and David Selby was so impressed by the results, that it was decided to hold further evening classes solely for the blind. Next we tackled flower arrangement. Colors, of course, were an obvious obstacle. Yet some flowers with so many differing leaves and petal shapes can be identified by touch, and hence the colors can be learned too. For example, since daffodils are unmistakable to the fingers, we knew immediately that we had a yellow flower. In addition, what we had been taught in the makeup and beauty class about matching colors was useful here. Applying all this knowledge and using the pin holders we were taught about, we came up with some quite respectable displays.

The following course, dressmaking, was an even bigger adventure. There had been dressmaking classes at my school, but I had never been allowed near the sewing machine, and such attempts as I had made unfailingly turned out badly. But the evening sessions under our two teachers, Irene and Hazel, were very different.

We started with basic techniques. We were all given small pieces of material and shown how to tack by making loops. We used wool or stronger thread instead of ordinary fine cotton so we could know what we were doing by touch. Then we were given skirt patterns. But instead of the ordinary kind of tissue patterns that are bought in shops, these were made of much thicker paper, almost the texture of wallpaper. Hazel and Irene had given this great thought and decided that with a stiffer paper we would be able to cut out the patterns ourselves. They had made dots an inch from the edge all around, so that once we had cut out the patterns we could fold them back and feel these dots in order to do the tacking. This was a fabulous innovation for the blind, and Hazel and Irene had achieved it by themselves wearing blindfolds and, by trial and error, discovering what a blind person might or might not be able to accomplish.

Next came work on the sewing machine. There were braille instructions on all the controls of the machine, and Hazel and Irene had also had a needle guard fitted, as well as a guide—in the shape of a long metal strip—to ensure that we put the material through straight.

Yet much as I admired all this, I was rather reluctant to make my first attempt. I heard the whirring of the machine as everyone else used it. Then Hazel came over and told me it was my turn. "Is it?" I said. "Surely there's someone else before me."

"No, everyone else has been. Come on, it won't bite you."

I went over to the machine and, feeling it gingerly all over, asked, "What if I get my hand under the needle and stitch my fingers?"

Hazel explained that the needle guard would protect me, so I had to start. Once I got my piece of material in the machine all went reasonably well. I found I had to be careful about the speed, which was controlled by a foot pedal. I chose a slow speed so I could feel what I was doing in time to avoid mistakes. At first I went a little crooked on the sewing, but Hazel was beside me to help. Eventually I mastered the technique, although that still didn't prevent me from making some blunders that would have instantly got me fired in a garment factory.

I suppose that the great thing about these evening classes was that they widened our confidence in our own capabilities—so much so that several of us got together and decided we should like to start a drama group for the blind in Nottingham. We knew there were similar groups in other places, so we went ahead. We obtained permission from our own local blind institution to hold rehearsals on their premises and found two drama teachers to help us.

At the first meeting, several problems presented themselves. We chose two short one-act plays and then had to decide how we were going to learn our parts. One of the teachers suggested that a recording could be made of the plays, so that we would be able to learn our lines from tape. This was fine. The next task was to work out how we were going to get around on the stage. Obviously we could not take our dogs with us. In the end it was decided that the stage would be exactly measured out for us, and the distances between each prop and piece of furniture. A strip of carpet would also be put at the front of the stage just before the footlights, to prevent us from falling into row A.

So in addition to learning our lines, we had to learn each movement, whether it was seven paces upstage and turn to the right, five paces from the wings and face outwards, or two paces to the left and exit stage right. We had great fun at rehearsals feeling our way around, particularly since we could hear our guide-dogs out front either sleeping and snoring, giving out great sighs and groans or puffing and heaving. We felt that they were transmitting collective criticism and commentary on the sight of us all fumbling about, fairly helpless without them.

At last we were ready for our first dress rehearsal. It was the evening before the actual show. We had been booked for two nights at a local amateur theater, and all the tickets had been sold. My part was this: I had to run onto the stage because someone had attempted to murder my aunt, rush forward, reach the carpet strip (and so know I was next to the bed by aunt was sitting on), sit down beside her and put my arm around her to comfort her, then go over to the telephone in the left-hand corner of the stage and dial the police. During rehearsals we had no telephone and simply pretended there was one. By the time of the dress rehearsal most of the props were in place, but I had been told a few days before that there would not be an actual telephone until the first night.

Unfortunately, things did not go as smoothly as we had hoped. I whisked onto the stage, shouting, "Aunty, I'm here, I'm here," and dashed over to her. I felt the carpet strip, turned round to sit on the bed, missed it completely, dragged her onto the stage with me, and we both sat in a heap, dying with laughter. To my horror, I heard more laughter—from out front—and it was only then that I realized an audience had been invited to watch the rehearsal. I was so embarrassed. When I had recovered and dusted myself down, I rushed over to where the phone was meant to be, pretended to pick it up and dial the police, and then made my exit to some rather puzzling murmurings from the audience.

I walked straight into the arms of the director backstage. She immediately hissed at me, "What were you pretending? What about the phone, then?"

"Well, I did that bit, I did that bit," I said.

"No, the phone was there," she said, "you fool. You were about an inch away from it, pretending to pick it up, and it was there all the time. The audience couldn't make out what you were doing."

But that was not the end of the evening's misfortunes. We all went on to take a curtain call, and the girl who had played my aunt had lost one of her slippers. When we were all on stage, she said, "Quick, I've lost one of my slippers. Help me find it." So when the curtain went up, there we were, on our hands and knees. I suppose stranger things have happened in the history of drama but I cannot imagine what they could be.

My evenings became even busier when I decided to take a second job in addition to my courses. One evening Don and I were discussing my finances (never very healthy) and I asked him if he thought there was anything I could do to earn a little over and above my wages from my job at the garage. I was well aware that not being able to see narrowed the field of opportunities, but I thought there must be something for me. As it happened, an Avon representative had called on Don that evening, and he suggested I could do that.

At first I was dubious. "Oh, Don," I said, "I really couldn't go around to people's houses and apartments trying to sell them things. And there's a lot of form filling involved that I couldn't do."

"Yes, you could," Don said, "and I could do the form filling for you. Why don't you call them and get one of their area representatives to come by?"

In the end I was persuaded, particularly since I could take a small tape recorder around with me and talk all the sales details into the microphone. I phoned the local Avon representative and she came by to tell me all about their selling scheme, and show me how to process the orders. I was in business.

I decided that I would limit myself, to begin with at least, to the three hundred apartments in my building and the adjoining ones; I knew how to get around them without much difficulty. So Emma and I set off, and I don't think she knew what to make of our stopping and knocking at every door. But things worked out well. The numbers on the doors were raised, and I could feel where I was. If people happened to be out when I knocked, I simply recorded their number on tape so I could call again the following evening.

The response was far better than I could have thought possible. I found a lot of people interested in the beauty products I was selling, and, very often, I was invited in for a cup of tea. But my success was due in no small part to Emma. Most of the people in the apartments had seen her out with me, and they welcomed the opportunity to say hello to her. Quite possibly they thought she looked as if she was trying to say, "Please buy something, or she won't be able to feed me tomorrow." I don't know if this was the case, but the orders came in very well. About once a week we would translate them off the tape, and Don would spend hours filling the forms in.

It was a rewarding extension to my life, and not only financially. Through the scheme I got to know a whole new circle of friends. In addition, I used to meet people who quite obviously rarely went out except to do the shopping, and who hardly had anyone to visit them. There were a lot of lonely people in those buildings, and I think they liked to see someone they could talk to.

It was astonishing, too, how I found myself able to help them in other ways. Because I had taken the makeup and beauty class, I was able to give advice. A surprising number of women used to want guidance about what shades they should wear. I used to ask, "What color hair have you got? What color eyes? What sort of tone would you say your skin is?" And then I would tell them what shades I thought best.

This really was wonderful and gave me even greater confidence. I thought, *Here I am blind, but I can help these people*. I hope not too many of them went around with the wrong color lipstick as a result!

9

SPREADING
THE WORD

After Emma and I had been together for about a year, I decided I wanted to become an official speaker on behalf of guide-dogs—to go around and tell people about their work and help raise funds. The first talk I ever did came about through Anita. She rang me from Grantham full of excitement.

"Guess what! I've got to come to Nottingham—my church is having a special charity function there in aid of guide-dogs! Could I stay with you? And do you think you could talk to them about Emma?"

I naturally agreed, and I felt on top of the world. When the day came, Emma and I got to the church, Anita met us, and we sat in one of the back rows. I could sense that there were a lot of people (about one hundred and fifty, I was told later). They started with prayers, and in the middle of a hymn I suddenly realized I was scared stiff. I thought, *What on earth persuaded you to do this sort of thing? You're going to have to stand up in front of all these people, and talk. You must be mad.* When the hymn came to an end, there was a terrible, expectant silence. I heard someone announcing that they had a speaker. Even worse, I heard my name.

They asked me if I would go to the front. With a thump in my heart I put Emma's harness on, took hold of the handle and told her to go forward. Up the aisle she went, taking me onto the platform. I had hoped for moral support from her, but it was fairly clear that none would be forthcoming. As soon as she turned and, obviously, caught sight of the audience, Emma walked behind me, curled up and put her nose through my feet in an attitude that plainly indicated, "You carry on doing whatever you have to; I'm well hidden."

I spoke, I suppose, for about five minutes. It seemed like five hours. I stuttered and stammered through the story of what had happened at the training center and tried to get across what Emma meant to me. The sole compensation was that, unlike sighted speakers, I could not be distracted by the faces in front of me. At the same time, I had no means of gauging their reactions. When I finally ran out of things to say I just stood trembling, and to my amazement there was a great burst of applause.

I could hardly believe it. Emma immediately leaped up from behind me, wagging her tail furiously (after all, the applause was for her). Then she took her harness, which was on the floor by my feet, and rushed away down the hall. She went from row to row to show how clever she was, and of course everyone was delighted. From that moment Emma was never shy of going to talks. As soon as I told her what we were about to do, there was no holding her. She would go at twice her usual rate.

All this required a lot of hard work keeping records, but here Don came in again. I bought large diaries, and he kept them up to date. On Sunday afternoons we would get the diary out, and Don would tell me all the information I wanted about the coming week. Then I would translate it through my braille machine and carry the separate braille instructions with me to the various lectures.

Only one thing ever deterred Emma from wanting to go to a talk, and that was rain. I would have to drag her, saying, "Come on, you won't get wet. You won't feel it with your great, furry coat." But Emma was aware, no doubt, that even if her coat protected her, she still had four big paws to slide about in the mud. Going to work, or more accurately, trying to persuade her to get me to work when it was raining, was a great performance. She would dig her paws in and refuse to move outside the building. I would beg, plead, cajole and even threaten her (in the politest possible way). Eventually she would move off, but I was often late for work.

When I started giving talks I was struck by the odd questions people used to ask at the end—for instance, "How do you find your clothes in the morning?" That stumped me, since I had never really thought about it. I would say, "Normally in a heap on the chair where I left them." I knew what they were getting at, but something that sighted people might imagine is an immense difficulty or inconvenience is really not that complicated when you are blind. You know where things are; it's your life.

The one thing I disliked about public speaking was the dinner that sometimes preceded the actual lecture. I remember one particularly dreadful occasion when I had to tackle a fruit cocktail that contained pineapple chunks. The chunks were very elusive, but I stuck to it, knowing by the lack of eating sounds around me that everyone was watching. It happened to be a warm summer evening, and I had on a rather low-cut dress. I finally captured a chunk and raised it in my spoon, when I suddenly became aware that it was attached to several other chunks in a kind of string. Worse, the shock of this made me drop the spoon—and the entire string of pineapple disappeared down my cleavage. Not the best start to an evening!

Well-meaning "help" was constantly being offered,

particularly on my arrival. I would be given a seat and told, "Now, don't move." I always think it strange that so many people regard the blind as rather dangerous and unstable explosive material which, if allowed the least chance of independent life and movement, may cause some sort of cosmic disaster. The blind are often treated as deaf as well, if not mentally defective. The admonition, "Don't move" was frequently a sort of military command: "DON'T MOVE!" I would sit there, tense and afraid lest someone suddenly grab me and forcibly propel me elsewhere. I would take Emma's harness off and then start to take my coat off. That was always fatal. The instant I stood up to do so, I was pounced on from all sides: "What do you want? What is it? Why are you moving?"

The thing that spurred me on through all these minor tortures was knowing that when I spoke, they would be the ones who could not move, and I would be able to demonstrate to them that I was just like any other human being, except that I could not see. When I stood up at the beginning, I could practically feel the tension generated at the thought of listening to someone who was blind. The last thing the audience wanted to do was to laugh. But somehow I succeeded in getting them to do just that, though it often took a little time.

Another of the rewarding results of my talks with Emma was that often the organizations we visited decided not only to give a donation to the Guide-Dog Association, but to try and raise the money to buy a guide-dog. The full cost of a guide-dog is five hundred pounds, including the puppy-walking, the training of the dog at the center and the training of the blind person with the dog. The cost of just training the dog at the center is about two hundred and fifty pounds.

When blind people go for their dogs they are not, of course, required to pay this sort of money (if they were, I should either have had to rob a bank, or would still be sitting at home saving up). All that is asked is fifty pence. This is just a pittance, but it enables blind people to have a dog no matter what their financial circumstances, and yet not feel that they are accepting pure charity. It also means that a lot of effort goes into raising money for guide-dogs, with many willing people devoting time and energy to it. So when my audience came up with the idea that they would like to contribute by paying for a guide-dog, I was always delighted.

One winter evening Emma and I went to speak in Newark, which is almost sixteen miles from Nottingham. When we got off the bus at seven o'clock, there was no one to meet us. I expected someone to drive us to the place at which I was giving the talk, as it was some way from the bus station. Emma and I walked up and down in the extreme cold. I felt my braille watch from time to time. Half past seven came, but no one arrived. Then I thought, *Have I made a mistake? Did I say the eight o'clock bus?* So we walked around a bit more. The eight o'clock bus duly rumbled in from Nottingham, but still no one arrived to pick us up.

By this time I was not only cold, but very hungry as well. Something had obviously gone wrong, and at this point I was overcome by hunger. "Emma," I said, "we're going for fish and chips. Can you find the scent?" So off we went, although I had never been to Newark before. Emma seemed much perked up by the prospect. We took a long time, endlessly searching the streets around the bus station, until, at last, I could smell the extremely alluring odor of fish and chips. I don't know whether Emma had led me to it, but she had a reward anyway and shared the food with me. Then we trailed back to the bus station, and a weary hour later were back in Nottingham.

I could not imagine what had gone wrong. It had been an utter waste of time. Even worse, I'd come away with no donation for the guide-dogs.

We had been indoors only a few minutes before the phone rang. A voice said, "Hello, this is Mansfield Young Wives here."

"Oh, yes."

"Where were you?"

"Where was I? When?"

"Tonight."

Then it dawned on me. At the time we had been stamping the pavements of the Newark bus station, there had been an impatient gathering of ladies stamping their feet in a hall in Mansfield. I suppose it was bound to happen sooner or later, but I could not apologize enough. What had happened, as it turned out when I checked with Don, was that he had quite firmly written "Mansfield Young Wives" in the book. But, by some aberration, I had transcribed Mansfield into braille as Newark!

One sort of talk I always enjoyed immensely was a Cub Scout or Brownie meeting. After adults, I found children so straightforward, unembarrassed and refreshing. Their questions were always imaginative, and they accepted me without reservation. I would never feel they were thinking, "Poor thing, she can't see." They took that for granted, and, in any case, were more fascinated by Emma and what she could do.

Typically, the thing children were most interested in was the way that Emma worked with me. They wanted a demonstration, but this created a difficulty. When I became an official speaker for the Guide-Dog Association, they stressed that on no account should demonstrations of this sort be given. The reasons were easy to understand: The dogs would be surrounded by people and all sorts of distractions; they would be working in artificial conditions, which would not be fair to them. This was fine as a theory. But Emma never appreciated it and seemed perfectly happy at a chance to show off. In fact, it would have taken someone with a stronger will than mine to deter her.

So I found that the best way of satisfying children's curiosity was a simple little act. From where I stood at the far end of the hall I would say, "I'm going to ask Emma to take me to the door, down the center aisle. But if you'd like to put some obstacles in my path, then you'll see how Emma does her job and takes me around them."

Emma was always thrilled when this moment arrived, since she enjoyed displaying her intelligence. Children would strew the aisle to the door with coats and other paraphernalia, and occasionally a chair or two. Emma outwitted their every move. If she could not find a clear path down the middle, she promptly took me another way, to immense applause.

On one particular evening with the Cubs, however, things took a slightly different turn. We completed the talk, Emma had done her demonstration and then I asked for questions. One very bright boy, who sounded about seven, was the first to stand up, and he asked, "Will Emma do anything anybody else tells her?"

"No, of course not," I said, totally unaware of what he was planning, after listening carefully to my talk about some of Emma's likes and dislikes.

"If I call her to come to me, won't she come?"

"No, I'm afraid she won't."

"Can I try?"

"Of course," I said confidently, "of course. Go ahead."

"Emma, Emma," he shouted. Emma remained at my side, and I imagine I probably had a silly grin on my face. Then he tried something different. He shouted at the top of his voice, "Emma, come on—butcher's!" And Emma moved so fast that she was down the hall in two seconds.

Although I liked talking to children, I was rather hesitant when an invitation to speak came from a school for handicapped children. When I spoke to the headmistress, she explained that many of the children were confined to wheelchairs, with diseases such as multiple sclerosis and spina bifida. All the children were to some degree crippled in their limbs and bodies. Some of them, apparently, had motorized chairs because their degree of paralysis was such that they were only just about capable of pressing the button to operate their wheels.

The headmistress asked me if I would talk to them because the children would love to see Emma and would like to know how a blind person coped with life. I was still apprehensive. I felt, I suppose, as a sighted person does at the prospect of being confronted with someone who is blind. But I decided I should go and made a booking.

When Emma and I arrived, I asked the headmistress, "Won't it be difficult to explain blindness? They're all so much more handicapped than I am. Will it mean anything to them?"

To my surprise she said, "We've talked about blindness in the classroom, and the children don't understand how you can get about when you can't see. They think it would be much worse to be blind than paralyzed."

I felt very strange, and could hardly agree. However, she suggested that we speak to the younger children first. I entered the classroom and then heard them coming in with their wheelchairs. They were all very quiet as I told them about Emma. She, I think, was rather puzzled about the wheelchairs. As a result, she was more subdued than usual during the talk. I was fascinated by the children's questions. They were very intelligent. "How do you tell the time?" one girl asked.

"Oh, that's easy. I've got a braille watch." I began to undo the strap of my watch.

"What's a braille watch?"

"I'll tell you—and if someone would like to come and get my watch from me you can pass it around. It looks like an ordinary wristwatch, but it has a sort of lid that flips up so I can feel the face. Now you all know about braille, which is the way blind people can read through feeling a system of dots on a page. On a braille watch there are dots—raised little bumps—instead of figures, and that's how I tell the time . . ."

As I was saying this, I heard the buzz of a motorized wheelchair and felt a hand take the watch. I heard the chair go away and a boy's voice saying, "Look, these are the dots . . . and that's how you feel to tell the time . . ."

"Can you read books in braille?" one child asked.

"Yes. I can get just about any book I want to read in braille. But most of the time I 'read' with the help of Talking Books. These are large cassettes that are played on a special machine. And when I'm listening to them I can do my housework too."

Next question: "How do you read your letters?" And a little girl's voice: "Do they come in braille?"

"No," I answered. "I'm afraid they don't. I wish they did. Some people send me cassettes so I can hear what they've got to say on my tape-recorder. But ordinary letters—like from the income tax bureau—I have to get someone to read them for me. If it's the income tax, I usually wish I hadn't found anyone to read for me."

There was some laughter. But I heard a whisper from a boy in a wheelchair close by, "Isn't that terrible? I'm glad I'm not blind." The others agreed. They all felt sorry for me, and it was very humbling.

Another institution for the handicapped I visited was Clifton Spinney, a rehabilitation center for blind people. Those who have recently lost their sight can go there for a one- or two-month course to help them reshape their lives without the aid of sight. Because of the gradual way I had lost what little sight I ever had, I always considered myself fortunate compared with people who had enjoyed perfect vision and then lost it. Naturally I had all the frustrations of being blind, but I had never at any point sat down and thought, *Last year I could see and now I can't; I shall never get used to this. What am I going to do?*

So, if I had been dubious about going to talk to handicapped children, I was doubly worried about the idea of speaking to the blind. One of the main reasons I lectured was to tell sighted people how normal blind people were—how they were able to cope and get on with their daily lives. And I explained and showed how I managed with Emma's help. How could I say this to these people?

Clifton Spinney was managed by a Mr. and Mrs. Spencer. Mrs. Spencer was sighted, but her husband was blind. It was good that a blind person was in charge, because no one knows better what the blind require than someone who cannot see. Mrs. Spencer was very kind. She picked me up and took me to the center, and, once there, led me along to the room where I was to give the talk, and where a blind audience was already waiting. She left me saying that her husband would be along shortly to introduce me.

I heard the door close. I sat on a little platform with Emma by me, and I realized that not only could I not see the audience, but they could not see me. The thought struck me forcibly, and I did not like it at all. I wasn't used to mixing with blind people. I had always chosen the company of sighted people, and if I had blind friends it was because I liked them personally, not because of, or with any allowance for, their not being able to see.

So I sat there, growing more and more apprehensive, and my throat going drier and drier, as I waited for Mr. Spencer. I could hear the audience chatting among themselves, and I noticed, not for the first time, that with the totally blinded—particularly those who have been recently blinded—there is a characteristic and very monotonous tone to their voices. It somehow reflects the idea that in losing their sight, all hope and interest in life has gone as well.

Then I heard Mr. Spencer come through the door. "Hello, Sheila. My name's Charles Spencer." I stood up and moved towards his voice, putting out my hand to shake his. We collided. My hand was somewhere on his jacket pocket, and his was near my left ear. I felt flustered and disheartened and thought, *This is what happens when you put blind people together*.

I started off the way I would begin one of my usual talks. "This is Emma," I said, and through the lead I felt Emma looking around for her usual response—a preliminary round of clapping. But there was no reaction whatsoever. What was wrong? Then it suddenly struck me that of course they couldn't see her. I decided to describe her but realized that wouldn't be good. I couldn't say what Emma was like in visual terms because I didn't really know, and to describe my own feelings about her wouldn't help them.

I was in a dilemma, and, since I had stopped speaking almost as soon as I had started, I detected the beginnings of restlessness in the blind audience—a shuffling of feet and coughing. Though they could not see it, I was also getting agitated. I tried another tack: "You've all heard of guide-dogs. I want to tell you about Emma, my guide-dog, and try to describe the kind of work she does for me, so that perhaps some of you, after you've heard what I've got to say, might want one yourselves."

This seemed to capture their attention. And as I went on to relate what Emma did for me—and sometimes did not do—I began to get a laugh or two. Finally, to my relief, the tension disappeared, and I no longer felt I was talking from the far side of some great chasm over which there was no bridge.

It was the most difficult talk I had ever done. And afterwards there was no sequence of questions, with one person asking after the other. Everyone shouted, and at times there were three questions in the air at the same time. This was not because newly blinded people are stupid or have no feeling for other people; it is because they feel cut off. They have suddenly been thrust on a dark island, and they have to do their best to get away from it. Many of them are still suffering the shock of losing their sight, of having to begin a completely different life, of having their main sense taken from them.

As the questions sorted themselves out, it became evident that the audience was particularly interested in guide-dogs, so Emma played her part in convincing them that, despite blindness, they could have real mobility and freedom. All the same I was truly glad to leave. This may seem a terrible thing to admit, but it's true. How thankful I was for Emma,

and for the start I had had in life. I could never
have worked there as Mr. Spencer did. It would
have been too close to home, too real. The problems
were all out in the open and being tackled. But in
his heart of hearts no blind person wants to admit
that there *is* a problem in not being able to see.

On the way home, I could not get that thought
out of my head. The experience had thoroughly
depressed me. The trouble was that having Emma
and the independence she gave me, almost convinced
me that I was really a sighted person. But, faced
with the blind people at Clifton Spinney, whom I
could not see and who could not see me, I had somehow realized what I myself must really have been
like to other people. The idea began to torture me.
Had I been living an illusion?

Don came by later. Before he arrived I had been
thinking in particular about him. I suddenly felt
that he must cover up a lot of what he really felt
about my blindness.

"How did it go?" I heard him say in his usual
cheerful way as he came in.

"Not very well," I answered.

Immediately he knew something was amiss.
"That's not like you, Petal. What's wrong?"

Petal was an affectionate name Don had chosen for
me.

"Oh, I don't know," I said, "I just feel terribly
low."

There was a silence, and I screwed up my courage
to ask what I really did not want to ask. "Don," I
said at last, "does it bother you that I can't see? I
mean, it must make a difference."

"Bother me?" he said, surprised. "No, it doesn't
bother me. Why should it? I don't understand.
You're . . . well, you're Sheila. Should there be a
difference?"

"Well, yes. I think there must be. That's what I felt when I was there with all those blind people—surrounded by them—and all of us, including me, having no idea what the others looked like. There must be something you'd prefer not to be the way it is now. Wouldn't it be easier for you if I could see?"

Don thought for a moment. "No, I can't really think of anything. I've never thought about it in that way. It doesn't make any difference in my feelings about you."

"But what about practical things? Like cooking, for instance . . ."

"Well, there are always the times when you give me peas and you've promised me beans."

"No, be serious. When we go out, do I really look okay? I mean, like other girls? You're not ashamed of me, are you, beause I can't see?" I asked.

He put his arm around me and said very gently, "Sheila, Petal, it's never crossed my mind. Ashamed of you? No, you look a million dollars, and always have." Then he laughed and added, "I'd tell you, you know, if you weren't." Switching into his imitation of John Wayne, he said, "I'm a hard man . . . and a man's gotta do . . ."

I could not keep from laughing and finishing the sentence for him. " . . . what a man's gotta do."

Don, as always, made the sun come out for me. He had given me his reassurance. The subject was never mentioned again.

10

EMMA SAVES
MY LIFE

People sometimes used to ask me how I knew if
Emma was not well. Obviously I could not see
whether she had a dry nose, had lost condition in her
coat, or was lacking her normal bounce. But I did
not need to see her, because of the extraordinary
bond between us. I could tell how she was as soon as
we got up in the morning and she had her first vigorous shake.

In addition, because she was a guide-dog she was
entitled to a free checkup every six months at the
vet. This was a good plan for anticipating any trouble before it became serious. There was only one
snag in this semiannual ritual: Emma loathed the
idéa.

I had to be slightly devious for her own good.
When preparing for a visit to the vet I would never
say anything to her, because Emma knew the street
the clinic was in as a familiar route. Her pace always
slackened on the approach to the vet's door, until she
was hardly putting one paw in front of the other.
Then, when she realized we were not actually making a visit, she would switch into top gear, and we
would zoom past as if late for an urgent appointment.

When the visit was a genuine one, I used to have
to wait until poor Emma had just about come to a
stop by the steps leading to the door, go up to them,

feel for the doorbell, hold on, and use gentle force to get her over the mat.

But there came the day, in between the regular checkups, when I first felt a small lump under her chest. I kept a check on it, and it seemed to be growing, so I decided I would have to take her to the vet. After we got over the inevitable dramatic performance on the doorstep, we found Dr. Davison on duty. He was a great lover of Labradors and was fond of Emma in particular.

He examined the lump and told me it should be removed, to be on the safe side. This meant I had to arrange to take Emma in early the following morning. Of course I was terrified that the lump might be malignant. I told the girls at work, and they were immediately sympathetic. They all agreed that once I had taken Emma to the vet, I ought to be picked up by the firm's car and taken home after the operation, and then have the rest of the week off to look after her. It did not work out quite like that, but it was a kind thought.

The following morning I took Emma, protesting as ever, to the clinic, and after Dr. Davison had given her the anesthesia, I stayed with her until she was asleep. One of the drivers from the garage, who was immensely understanding about the whole thing, took me to the office, where I waited the two hours. My thoughts were in turmoil: terrible anxiety for Emma, mixed with anticipation of the problems that would be involved in getting about without her to lead me. The lump on her chest was just where the harness went, and she would certainly not be able to wear it for a little while.

Those hours were quite extraordinary. Not only was I worried because Emma was at the clinic under anesthesia, but I instinctively kept feeling her bed under the switchboard, listening for her, expecting to feel her touch my knee with her nose. It was like having left part of myself somewhere else. I couldn't bear the thought of anything happening to Emma.

At last twelve o'clock came, and again my chauffeur from work took me down to the vet, parked, and waited for me to fetch Emma. Dr. Davison soon brought her to me. She had not long recovered consciousness, and I could hear by her walk she was shaky on her feet. But what a welcome! The way she wagged her tail was nearly making her fall over; I heard her slip and slide about as she saw me. Even in that state she made an immense fuss over me.

When I'd thanked the doctor, I clipped Emma's lead around her collar ring instead of putting her harness on, and we made our way out. I went very slowly—as much for my own sake as Emma's—but when the door was opened for us, Emma turned, took hold of the lead about halfway up, and walked in front of me. I was not very sure why, but then I realized that we were at the top of the steps and she was telling me that because she was not wearing her harness, she could not help me in her normal way; instead, she was taking the lead in her mouth to guide me.

We got home, and Emma slept peacefully in front of the fire for most of the day while the anesthesia wore off. But I was still worried, wondering what the news about the lump would be. I had a nightmare that I was in the middle of Nottingham, alone, with no Emma and no Don, and there were people, noise and confusion all around me. I was so terrified I could not move.

Two days later, there was good news in the mail: the results from the laboratory were negative. It had only been a fatty lump, and there was nothing malignant. My relief was boundless.

During the period when Emma could not work, I

felt quite helpless. I suppose I might have been able to get to the shops without Emma, but I really did not have the courage even to try to set foot outside the door without her. She had been with me for so long the idea was inconceivable. Fortunately, she was back in harness fairly soon, because the small wound healed quickly. As we strode off down the street together, it seemed incredible to be free again. And knowing what it was like without that freedom made the feeling even greater.

How thankful I had to be for Emma was brought home to me again some weeks after this. Going through town one day, she took me to a crossing at a busy point. I heard a bus or a truck pull up to let us cross. I gave Emma the signal to go forward. We had taken only a step or two before Emma stopped, and began to back away, tugging on the harness. I could not understand what she was doing and entirely forgot to trust her. "Emma, come on. It's all right. They've stopped for us," I urged. She would not move, however, and I thought I must step out to show that everything was clear—because I could hear the engine of the bus or truck safely idling and waiting for us. So I stepped forward. Then Emma did the most incredible thing. She made a sort of leap in front of me and almost knocked me back into the gutter. At the same moment I suddenly heard a growing noise and a car roared across the street ahead of me. Another inch forward and I would have been killed, if Emma had not stopped me.

The whole incident took only seconds, but I just stood there on the crossing, totally petrified. I heard the engine next to me stop and the sound of a cab door sliding open.

"Are you all right?" an anxious voice asked. It was a bus driver.

"Yes," I said.

"I've never seen anything like it. I couldn't get his license number. He must have been doing fifty miles an hour."

"Yes," I said, still too shaken to react any more.

Then the driver added, "I've never seen anything like your dog, either. It's lucky she did that. You've got a good dog there, Miss."

With that, he got back into his bus, started up, and drove off. Emma, in turn, was anxious to be going, and as she trotted placidly along I kept thinking of the driver's words. Yes, I certainly did have a good dog. She had saved my life.

Around this time, one aspect of life that was beginning to worry me a little was the fact that the apartment had no garden for Emma to run in. There were parks not far away where I took Emma for her free run. But this was not the same as being able to open the door at any time to let her out. Nor was it the same as Emma having her own patch of lawn and her own boundaries. I determined to try to move.

After a great deal of telephoning and talk with the project officials, I at last succeeded in persuading them to let me exchange the apartment for a small bungalow. It was prefabricated and getting on in years, but it had a little garden that Emma took to at once, scampering all over and snorting in the hedges on the trail of long-vanished cats.

Don helped me move this time, and I was soon settled in. Once there, I happily realized that I could again have a cat. Ever since I had taken Emma to the vet one day and we had sat next to someone with a litter of Siamese kittens, I had wanted one. So I bought a male kitten, a flamepoint, and named him Ohpas, the Siamese word for "sunlight." Later I purchased another to keep him company, a regal feline named Ming. Both of them adored Emma, and she, in turn, took particularly to Ming, recognizing in her a kindred spirit.

But the arrival of the Siamese served only to inflame Emma's only great and irresistible temptation—food. Don told me that when feeding time came, Emma would lie with her nose on the carpet like an alligator in the shallows, awaiting her chance for the remains in the cats' bowls.

To this end she set to work moulding Ming into a partner in crime. Emma's greed had only one major obstacle in the house: the drainboard, which she was unable to reach. Ming was accordingly trained to come to the rescue. I have no idea how it was done. But plainly Emma taught her to get up on the drainboard (with Siamese silence and stealth) and throw down any scraps, or even tastier prizes, for Emma to eat. Don used to watch this extraordinary performance (when they were unaware they were being observed), and he told me that Ming was mainly concerned in getting the food to Emma, reserving hardly a morsel for herself.

Having one male and one female cat in the household produced an inevitable result: a litter of Siamese kittens. I was told they were unusually beautiful, so I decided to take them to cat shows. I enjoyed the competitions, and gradually my walls became covered with commendation certificates.

Soon I had another scare about Emma. Once a year she had to be passed fit to do her work by the Guide-Dog Association. She was due for her examination, and because she was nearly ten years old I was a little concerned. I began to fear that she might be retired simply on the grounds of her age. So many of my friends who had guide-dogs of about that age were being advised to retire them and go for new dogs. I would often talk about my apprehensions to Don, and he would say, "Oh, there's no need

to worry. Even if she had to retire, I can take her
with me to my clinic every day. She'll be all right.
She'll be quite happy." Well, possibly she might, I
thought, but it was a desolating prospect to have to
face.

I knew that I would not really be losing Emma,
but the idea of any other dog doing her job, of being
in harness with me, seemed so disloyal. It was un-
thinkable. I remembered how Dotty had wept my
first evening at the training center, all those years
ago. Faced with the same situation myself, I really
understood how heartbroken she had been at having
to go for a replacement for her first dog.

The letter from the Guide-Dog Association arrived and said that the trainer would come to my
home on Thursday at two o'clock. I was dreading
what he might decide, even though rationally I knew
that Emma worked as well as any younger dog. She
was sprightly, as full of energy as she had ever been.

He arrived on the dot of two, and Emma was on
her best behavior as I put her harness on and braced
up to the task. I hoped so much that he would not
see anything that I had not been able to detect in
her work. "I'll go through town," I said, "if it's all
right with you; it's our usual route to the bus station."

Mr. Soames, the trainer, was a pleasant man, and
he said that was fine. We had not picked the best of
days. There was a great wind that beat against us
when we started out, and shortly there was a flurry
in our faces. But we went on towards the bus stop,
and Emma seemed the least troubled of any of us.
She trotted along the pavement in her normal fashion. Then, at one busy crossing, I could hear two
dogs growling and barking at each other. Emma ignored them completely and crossed right by them,
putting on an even faster pace than usual. By the

time we were at the bus stop and the end of the test, I was exhausted.

I waited for the decision. I had half made up my mind that if it went against us I was going to say I refused to have Emma retired. Then Mr. Soames said, "I saw Emma about four or five years ago."

"Oh, did you?" I asked.

"Yes. You haven't been putting brown boot polish on her nose, have you?"

"Boot polish? No, of course not." (What was he driving at, what was he going to say?)

"Well, it's very strange. She hasn't gone a bit gray, you know."

"I know. Everyone tells me she still looks very young."

"She does," said Mr. Soames. "She does look very young."

I had begun thinking. *He's leading up to tell me that she looks young, but he knows that she's going on in years* . . . But Mr. Soames did not say any more, and I suddenly grasped his meaning.

"You mean," I said, "you're not going to tell me to retire her?"

"Retire her?" he said, sounding quite surprised. "Retire Emma? No, no, of course not. Goodness me." Then he laughed. "I should think the way she's shown us all up today she'll still be working when she's eighteen!"

I felt like shouting my elation. I said good-bye to Mr. Soames, and Emma and I headed for home. On the way back I stopped to buy her a new rubber bone. And that evening Don and I went out to celebrate.

Not long after this we had an even greater cause for happiness. At long last all the uncertainty, the lonely nights, and five years of waiting were over. Don was free to marry me.

Yet I did not want to rush out to tell the world and have a big elaborate wedding. I felt that our love was a very private thing, and I wanted to share it with only the very closest of family and a friend or two. When I called to invite them, they were absolutely thrilled at the news.

"What shall I wear?" I asked Don.

"Well, Petal, it's up to you, it really is."

"It's got to be something green," I said, because I associated green with spring, and with all things that were fresh and lovely.

The next day I went shopping with my mother. She searched through countless dresses before selecting one that she liked the look of, and I liked the feel of. But there was Emma to consider, too. I thought that perhaps she ought to have a bow. But then Don and I decided it would not be dignified for our maid of honor.

The morning of our wedding finally came. It was cold as Emma and I sat in the taxi on the way to the registry office, but I could feel the sun warm on my face, like the feeling I had inside. Emma had been given special permission to attend, particularly because I had pointed out that I refused to be married without her.

I found I was trembling as I pushed open the heavy door. I could not believe it was happening, that Don would be mine forever. Inside, I heard his voice call out, "Hello, darling." He took my hand. "You look beautiful," he said.

As Don held my hand, I felt he was trembling too, and I could hardly say the simple words "I will" in front of the registrar. Emma must have sensed the extreme tension, for halfway through the service her cold, wet nose nuzzled my left hand, as if in moral support.

Then it was all over, and as Don and I walked out hand in hand, I felt the confetti and my mother and father embrace me. But I do not think I was really aware of what was happening around me, or even what had in fact happened, until I heard Graham come up. He said, "Well, Sheila, it's Mrs. Hocken at last." Then I knew it was really true. I did not have to pinch myself to see if I was in fact dreaming.

Yes, I said to myself, thinking fleetingly of my long-ago assumption that I would never marry. *Mr. and Mrs. Hocken.* It was what mattered most in the world. And at the little bungalow that now was our home, the corks popped far into the night in celebration of that joyous fact.

11

FRESH HOPE

One bleak January day in 1975, Emma and I had just arrived home from work, and as I put the key in the latch of the front door I heard the telephone ringing. For some reason the key did not work properly, and I remember tugging and turning it impatiently and hoping the phone would not stop. When I finally got inside and lifted the receiver, I heard Graham's voice.

Graham, as I've mentioned, has a similar eye complaint to mine, but despite having lost the use of one eye entirely when he was very young, he always had, unlike me, some residual vision in the other eye. In addition he was constantly seeking means to improve the sight he had. He was calling now to tell me about his latest efforts.

He told me he had gone to a new optician in order to try to get some contact lenses, and the optician had advised him to see a specialist named Dr. Shearing, with the advice, "This man is really good. There are a lot of new techniques that he knows all about." So, despite the reluctance of our family to have anything to do with specialists or eye surgery because of bitter experience in the past, Graham had seen Dr. Shearing, who was an ophthalmic surgeon.

"How did you get on? What happened?" I asked excitedly.

"Well," he said, "I have good and bad news. He said it would be fairly simple to operate and remove the lens that my cataract is on, but in my case, he wouldn't really like to take the risk because there's only something like an eighty-five per cent success rate. Because I've got some vision, he said it would be a terrible thing if the operation wasn't successful. He wants me to wait a bit longer to see if anything new develops. Anyway, the older I am, the easier the operation is, because as you know, the lens hardens with age, and the easier it is to break and bring away without any danger of messing up the rest of the workings of the eye."

I felt a bit deflated, but then he went on, "I still think that you could go and see him. He's a very nice guy, practical but extremely sympathetic. You never know what he might be able to do for you."

I thought that Graham was right. What would be the harm in just going and presenting my case to this specialist? I phoned the following day and made an appointment, and I was surprised, when I put the phone down, to find that I felt quite nervous.

I suppose the reason was that I had, on a conscious level, accepted the fact of being blind. But underneath, like all blind people, I had *never* accepted it. There is always a small voice somewhere at the back of the mind insisting, *I've got to see. I can't go on living like this.* But that voice always has to be strangled, suppressed, put out of mind, because if you heed its message you will never be anything more than a ragbag of regret, and unable to take your part in the world, a part limited by the fact that you can't see.

I'm always distressed when I meet people who have lost their sight and never bothered to learn braille. I say "never bothered," but it is the wrong phrase. If I said they were "unable" that would also be wrong. What is behind their attitude is a dogged, misguided lack of acceptance of the facts as they are. Instead, they prefer to dream that they are going to have their sight restored somehow. Their conversation is always of the last specialist they went to or the operation they are going to have. It is all so understandable, but sad, because such active hopes simply prevent the day-to-day business of getting on with life on the terms that have been dictated. I always tried to work along the lines of acceptance. It was only when I thought of having sight again that the frustration and sheer hatred of being blind arose. And here I was, shaking, because those very hopes were rising in me.

I had to wait three weeks before going to see Dr. Shearing. The hopes got bigger, and the hatred of blindness more intense. My imagination ran wild. When I made the appointment I said to Don, "Well, that's it. Isn't it fabulous? I'm going to start saving. I'll be able to buy a car—I'll be able to go anywhere I want." The idea of having to pass a driving test never even entered my head. I went on, "I'll be able to join the public library. I can't wait to look through all those shelves. I'll be able to read anything I choose."

"Yes," said Don. "Wonderful." But at the same time, his voice did not sound as enthusiastic as I thought it should.

"What's the matter?" I asked.

Then he tried to tell me, as tactfully and gently as he could, not to build my hopes up too much. He wanted to be encouraging but did not want me to be let down if things didn't work out. I knew what he was saying. I heard his words, which were meant to protect me. Yet I still let my excitement get the better of me. *Yes, it might not work. But what if it did?* It was a prospect I could not resist, although I knew my dreaming must have been difficult for Don.

At last it was time for my appointment. Graham said he would go with me, and we agreed to meet at the bus station. When the bus arrived, Emma led me on, found a seat for me, and then, as always, lay quietly under the seat, while my brother sat down next to me. Graham is not a great one for small talk and chat, so we sat there not saying anything much as the bus moved off. It was an hour's journey from Nottingham, and as we rode along, all sorts of imaginings about the possibility of seeing began to stalk through my mind.

I suddenly thought about Emma, and for the first time my worries about having to have another dog because of Emma's age were quieted. I realized that if I could see, she would not have to guide me; I would be able to take her for a walk like other dogs. The partnership of nine years would not have to be wrenched apart.

Graham led the way to Dr. Shearing's office and said he would leave me there because he had some shopping to do. We rang the bell, and he said, "I'll be back in about half an hour. All the best."

The door opened, and I smelled that strangely clean, antiseptic smell mixed with floor polish that belongs to doctors' offices. A receptionist led me into the waiting room, and I sat alone, Emma beside me. I was not there very long before I heard the door open, and a quiet voice said, "Mrs. Hocken?" I stood up. "Would you come this way, please?" Emma guided me into what sounded like a very big room with wall-to-wall carpeting. I felt a fire in front of me; Emma had headed for it right away.

"Well, lassie," I heard a voice say, "what can I do for you?"

"I want to know if you can possibly help me."

There was a silence during which I could hear the clock ticking somewhere away to my left, and the gas fire hissing. I realized afterwards that Dr. Shearing must have been surprised to see someone led into his consulting room by a guide-dog.

Then, at last he said, "Mmmm. Well. Would you care to have a seat?"

I told Emma to find a chair. I felt it, took her harness off, and sat down.

"What's your name, then?"

I thought, *What a terrible memory. He can't even remember my name.* "Sheila Hocken," I said.

"No, no. This lovely creature sitting beside you."

"Oh," I said, "Emma."

"Emma. Yes. That suits you." And I heard him patting her. "I used to have two boxers, you know."

"Boxers? I love boxers." I asked him about them, and he told me all the details. They had died of old age. "Haven't you a dog now?"

"Mm. I have a bloodhound. Very willful blood-hounds are, you know, very willful."

I was enjoying talking about dogs but was beginning to wonder if we were skirting the main topic because he could not bring himself to ask the ques-

tions. I was growing anxious, but at last he asked me
to tell him all about my eyes.

I explained about the hereditary factor, and how
his seeing my brother and holding out a wonderful
opportunity for him had led me to come along. He
was very quiet as I went on.

When I had finished, he led me over to another
chair and put drops in my eyes to dilate the pupils
so that he could make a better examination. "I'll
leave you here for a little while so the drops can
work. I'll be back in about ten minutes." I heard
him go out of the room and close the door behind
him. Once again all I could hear was the clock and
the hiss of the gas fire. This time, Emma's sleeping
deep breaths were added, keeping up an odd coun-
terpoint with the tick of the clock. I could hear nothing from outside, and in the air I could smell just
the faintest aroma of cigar smoke.

He came back in what seemed to me less than ten
minutes. I felt him examining my eyes. He hemmed
and hawed a bit and then said decisively, "Come and
sit in a more comfortable chair." He took me back to
where I had been sitting before, and I heard him
making a fuss of Emma again, and from her little
snorts and growls I knew she was enjoying it. I was
longing to ask him what he had seen, what he
thought. But he just went on talking to Emma, telling her how beautiful she was. I became impatient,
but sat and waited.

"Well, lassie," he said finally. "What do you expect
I'm going to say?"

What did I expect? I didn't know. I couldn't
think. It was too overwhelming even to frame into
words what I so much wanted to hear. I said, "I
don't know. I was hoping, after my brother had been
to see you . . ."

"Well," said Dr. Shearing, "you know you've got

cataracts. But you're aware of this retina problem, aren't you?"

"Yes," I said rather lamely, "I do remember that. But what does it entail? Could you explain it?"

"I'll have to try. Now, you have cataracts, and obviously we're talking about congenital cataracts, where the retina, depending on the thickness of the cataracts, has not had a proper chance to develop. The thicker the cataracts, the less chance of the light's reaching the retina, and the less chance the retina has of developing properly.

"If the cataracts are very thick, the light can't get to the back of your eye, and as this has happened in your case, your retinas won't have developed."

"Yes," I said, my heart already sinking, "I understand. But isn't there anything you can do?"

He sat there for what seemed an age. I felt my mind becoming cold and empty, and strangely numb. I was incapable of rational thought, or any reaction beyond suddenly wanting to get up and go.

But then, to my utter surprise, he said, "Yes. I think there is. At least I could have a try. I could try removing the lens, or part of the lens, and see what success we have."

Excited, I asked immediately, "What sort of sight would I have? How much would I be able to see?"

His reply brought me straight back to earth, to the chair bounded by darkness. 'It's a terribly difficult question, lassie. I just don't know."

"Well," I said, because I had to know as much as possible despite the consequences, "if you did an operation and it was a success, would I still need Emma to guide me? Would I be able to read, for instance?"

"Oh," he said, "I think you'd still need Emma, and as for reading—well, lassie, I don't work miracles."

I was desolate. All those thoughts of what I

would—not even might—be able to do evaporated. I had expected a miracle, and I should have known better.

Dr. Shearing was a gentle, thoughtful man, and he must have seen the disappointment in my face. He said in a voice full of compassion, "Now, lassie, I couldn't promise you anything. You wouldn't want a promise from me that you yourself knew might not be fulfilled. We might give you some sight, we might not. Well, it would be worth a try, wouldn't it? Anything would be better than what you have at the moment, don't you agree?"

Of course, he was right. "Yes," I said, "anything at all would be better than nothing. I've got nothing to lose."

When I asked him why Graham's case held out the possibility of perfect sight, he explained that my brother's cataract was very slight compared with mine, and the retinas were not retarded. He went on to say that my retinas, because of underdevelopment, would not pick up detail. They simply lacked the facility.

I said, "Well, I must come in for an operation."

"There's no need to rush into it, lassie. Go home, think about it, and let me know on Monday."

I felt utterly dejected. When Dr. Shearing had gone, Graham, who had already returned, asked, "Well?"

"Well—nothing."

"Nothing? What do you mean? He must have said something."

We walked back to the bus station and I told Graham more or less everything that had passed between me and the doctor.

Graham gave a great sigh. "What a terrible shame. I thought maybe you would stand to gain almost perfect sight."

"Well," I said, "obviously not."

"What are you going to do?"

"I'm going to have the operation." I got on the bus, and Emma went to sleep under the seat as we rumbled back to Nottingham. Neither Graham nor I spoke.

When Don came home he tried to comfort me, but I sat there feeling sentenced for life. Until that afternoon there had always existed some hope, deep down, that one day things might be better. I had to have the operation, but I also had to face the strong probability that I would be blind for the rest of my life. Then Don came to the rescue. He reminded me that when I was much younger and could see a little I had been to eye specialists who had forecast that I would be totally blind. But though they had been nearly right—and right for all practical purposes—what they had meant was that I would be in a black void, whereas I could still distinguish darkness from light. That ability was of no use to me, but I had it.

The thought began to cheer me. What if Dr. Shearing was wrong, too? In any case, I realized, no specialist is going to promise a miracle. So when I went to bed I was a little more cheerful because of Don's love and encouragement.

On Monday I called Dr. Shearing and said I would have the operation. When I put the phone down, my hopes were still alive.

12

THE OPERATION

The letter telling me that the operation had been scheduled arrived nine months after my visit to Dr. Shearing. It gave me only four days' notice, and this was a relief. I had to organize everything so quickly for my stay in the hospital that there were few moments left over for brooding or yearning.

I was to go in on Wednesday, September 3. The day before was a little like the last day of the year, when one keeps thinking, *This is the last time I shall do this in nineteen-seventy-whatever.* At the office everyone wished me luck, and one of the girls came up to me and said, "Wait, wait till you come back, you'll be able to see us all. I wonder what you'll think?"

"I don't know," I said. "Won't it be fantastic?" My friend was more confident than I. But I could not pretend that I had not thought countless times about the visual identities of the people I knew so well by their voices. I had an impression of all their personalities and what the office was like, and I had my own images of what everything and everybody looked like, but it was odd to think that I might be walking out of there for the last time as a blind person.

When I got home, I heard Emma lap at her bowl of water and patter off into the living room. I thought, *That might have been the very last time you had to take me anywhere, Emma.* Then I followed her, sat down, and starting thinking of the final details involved in going into the hospital.

Don, of course, would be looking after Emma. He was going to take her to the clinic with him, and she would accompany him in the car on his rounds and wherever he went. Because of the short notice the hospital had given, there had been no chance to arrange time off for him to take me in and obviously he could not cancel his patients' appointments. Instead, Deirdre, the wife of Don's partner, was going to take me.

The following morning I was quite nervous, and before Don left I said, "Now you won't forget to give Emma her biscuits, will you? Oh, and don't forget her bowl of milk in the morning."

Don replied patiently, "You know I'll look after Emma. Don't worry. She's almost as much a part of me as she is of you."

And I knew that was true. Then he kissed me, and said, "Well, the best of luck." I said something flippant, like "I'll need it." But the words only masked the feelings that we both knew were overwhelming us both. Just as he was taking Emma out of the door, I said, "I don't know how I'm going to face it without the pair of you to back me up."

"Now don't *worry.* Everything will be all right. And I'll be there with you every night."

With that, he and Emma were gone. I heard the car start up and move away, and I felt so alone. I had never been parted from Emma in nine years, except when she had had her operation, and that was only for two hours. Without Don and his constant reassuring presence, any idea that the operation *might* be a success ebbed away.

Fortunately, Deirdre was not long in arriving, and she was full of kindness and remarks that restored my confidence. My suitcase was already packed. We chatted happily as we drove along. At the hospital she checked me in and took me to the ward, and she left me with the same words Don had used. "Well, the best of luck."

"Thanks, Deirdre," I said.

I was met at the ward by a young student nurse, a very pleasant girl named Jasmine. "Oh, yes. Mrs. Hocken," she said. "Would you come this way?" The sound of her footsteps began to recede, and I thought, *Help, what do I do?* She obviously didn't know I could not see, and so I stood there feeling foolish, and wondering who was looking at me. After she returned I explained my situation and I think she was more embarrassed than I was. I put out my hand to take her arm.

When we reached my bed, Jasmine asked if I would get undressed. "Can you manage?" she asked.

"Yes, thanks," I said and added, "Do I have to get into bed?"

"Oh, no," said Jasmine, "just put your dressing gown on. Patients only go to bed at night here, because there's no one really ill. You can stay in the ward if you like, or go into the day room."

"Good," I said.

Then she began, "What about magazines . . ." and stopped herself with, "oh, I'm sorry, you can't read. I really am sorry."

"That's all right," I said, "but I can read. I've brought some braille magazines with me."

Jasmine, as it turned out, had never seen braille before, and she was fascinated. She watched my fingers as I read from one of the magazines and explained how braille works, with its contractions and abbreviations.

"Well," she said. "I don't think I could do that,"

and she took me down the ward to the day room. On the way, she showed me around the ward so that I could get to know how many steps there were from my bed to the bathroom, how many beds were on each side of the ward and so on.

I had two days to wait before my operation: the Wednesday of my arrival, and the Thursday. Dr. Shearing came to see me on the second day. I knew he was in the ward because of the faint aroma of cigar smoke that penetrated from beyond the doors. (He must have gone into Sister's office to have a smoke.) He stayed for a while in the course of his normal rounds and told me a little more about the operation—what had been done in the past and what the newer techniques of eye surgery entailed. With a young patient the cataract is relatively soft and sticky, and attempts to make holes through the lens or pull the lens away often resulted in detachment of the retina. Even when this had not happened, holes had been made in the lens that healed as scabs and so the patient ended in a worse state than when he had gone into the hospital.

Dr. Shearing explained that he intended to take the middle part of my lens away. The lens, he said, was like an onion, with layer after layer of tissue, so taking the middle part away and leaving the outside would protect the retina and let the light through the middle. He had no idea, of course, what my retina would be like, beyond the fact that it would not be developed. It was believed that with this kind of retina detailed vision was not possible.

I loved talking to him, and though it still did not make me any less scared, I had a kind of confidence in him. Don came in to see me on both evenings, and on the Thursday night I remember saying to him, "Well, this time tomorrow, it will all be over."

"Yes," said Don, not concealing his anxiety very well, "I'll be thinking of you all day."

Beyond that, not much passed between us apart from talking about what Emma had been doing and how good she had been with Don in the car. For most of the time we just sat there and sort of hoped together.

I went to sleep very easily that night, and then, on Friday morning, I woke up with an extraordinary sensation of being on top of the world. All the worries seemed to have disappeared. I knew this was the day, yet instead of being scared, I simply thought, *I'm glad it's here, and I'm not worried.*

At about nine o'clock I was taken down to the operating room, and I still could not get over this feeling. It was not quite happiness, but a great feeling that something really momentous was about to happen, and that I need not be afraid. When the anesthetist gave me a final injection, I remember simply trailing off, saying to myself, *This is the moment . . . the moment of . . .* And the words never materialized.

I came to in the ward. My first thought was, *It's over, thank goodness, it's over.* But I knew I would be bandaged over the eyes, so I was not expecting to be able to know immediately whether the operation had worked. Most of all, I was feeling thirsty. I felt as if I could have drained a reservoir. Yet I was not able to muster the effort to ask for a drink. I lay still, vaguely hearing other people coming and going and familiar hospital noises. After about an hour, I at last managed to say, "Could I have a drink, please?"

Don was coming in to see me that evening, and I remember making a great effort not to be doped so that I would appear reasonably sensible and alert for him. I would know when he had arrived by his footsteps approaching the bed. But all I heard were the nurses' footsteps, all different: Annette, Anne, Jasmine, Alison, Linda, and the head nurse, whom everyone called Sister.

Sister was a tremendous character who had not been there on the day I arrived. Head nurses make or break a hospital ward, and this one certainly made it. Far from being a fire-breathing martinet, she spread an infectious goodwill. She exploded into the room, bubbling all over. She kept everyone laughing and joking, and made the ward an enjoyable place to be.

When I finally recognized Don's footsteps I felt relieved. His presence quieted the thoughts perpetually at the back of my mind: *Has it worked? Hasn't it worked?*

Don sat by me and asked, "When will they take the bandages off? When will you know?"

I said, "Monday," and we both knew what a long weekend lay ahead.

But it passed, as all time passes. My parents and Graham came to see me on Saturday, and all of us were facing possibilities we couldn't translate into adequate phrases.

"I bet you can't wait until Monday."

"No, I can't."

So much was unspoken behind this exchange—a family history of blindness, of pain and hope.

Don, when he visited again, could not hide his feelings. In a very loving way he said, "Well, you know, if it hasn't worked and you can't see, it won't matter as far as we're concerned, will it? It's never made any difference in the past, and there are still so many things to do together."

Time went by slowly in the ward, spaced out by the set hours for meals, temperature taking, pills and sleep. On Sunday evening, Don was at my side again. 'Now, you'll ring me, won't you?" he asked.

"Of course."

"As soon as you know."

"Of course I will." I knew that he wanted so much to be there at the time the bandages were taken off, and to know as soon as I did, but he couldn't because of his practice.

When it was time for him to go, he said, "Oh, I hope it's worked, I hope it's worked . . ." Then, after a pause, he added, "They're such insufficient words, aren't they?"

"No, they're not," I said. "I know just what you mean. The next time you come in, we really will know."

And from then, from the time he left on Sunday night, there began seemingly endless hours of waiting, an interminable countdown to the conclusion I could not escape.

The hours from eight o'clock Sunday evening to ten o'clock Monday morning would normally go in a flash, a brief interval from supper to going to work. But now time seemed stretched on the rack, and I with it. The minutes and seconds went on and on and on. I kept feeling my watch. I could hear it clicking away, but never fast enough.

In the bed on one side of me was May, and on the other side Muriel. Both had been very good to me, and I heard Muriel, quite late, call over to me, "I can hear you feeling your watch. Don't worry. Morning will be here soon enough, you know. Try to get some sleep, Sheila."

But sleep was out of the question. I felt my watch again. It was seven minutes past twelve. Past midnight. It was Monday! . . . Now my watch told me it was ten past one, then eight minutes to two, and then I think I did at last sleep a little, because next it was six o'clock, and the nurses were coming around to take temperatures and bring the early tea.

I sat up. *Another four hours*, I thought. *Four whole hours.* I lit a cigarette, which was not strictly permitted, but I was so nervous I hardly cared. Perhaps because everyone realized what I was going through, I wasn't asked to stop.

At eight o'clock—several cigarettes later—breakfast came. I did not want it, but I thought, *I must eat it. It will pass the time. It will take another fifteen minutes away.* All too soon I was down to the toast and marmalade, and it was still only ten after eight. *What*, I thought, *am I going to do for nearly another two hours?*

Muriel came over and asked, "Are you all right?"

I said, "Yes, I'm fine, but I think I shall go mad before ten o'clock. I just can't wait. It's terrible."

"Why don't you go and have a bath? It'll fill in some of the time."

"That's a good idea," I said. *If I have a bath*, I thought, *it might take half an hour away—if I take my time.* But, though I tried to be leisurely, I found that I took only about ten minutes. I must have been hurrying without noticing it.

When I got back in the ward I began pacing up and down, and again Muriel came over. "Do you want to go to the day room? We can go in there and listen to the radio," she said.

"No, I don't think I want to go down there. Thanks all the same."

The reason, I told her, was that the treatment room where my bandages would be removed was just outside the door of the ward, but the day room was at the opposite end, and at ten o'clock I wanted to be as near as I could to hear my name called. Muriel and May then brought a table up to my bed so that we could all sit there and pass the time that way. They were a great help in keeping my mind off the approaching question.

Every five minutes I kept feeling my watch, and, in between, I smoked endlessly. Muriel lectured me in a friendly sort of way about the amount I was smoking. I said, "I know I shouldn't, but I must do something." It was nine-forty by then, and I had to get up and walk up and down again. My stomach kept turning over; always at the back of my mind there was that warning from Dr. Shearing, "I don't perform miracles, lassie."

Then I heard Annette coming down the ward, and I called to her, "Have you started the dressings yet?"

"Not yet," she said, "but we won't be long—and don't worry, we'll make sure you're first." I felt my watch again. The dots must have been nearly worn away. There was only ten minutes to go.

13

THE BANDAGES COME OFF

When at last Sister came into the ward and called, "Sheila," I just sat there. Everyone has heard of people being paralyzed with fear or apprehension, and I suppose this is literally what happened. I was sitting just inside the ward, not more than a few yards from the treatment room, and I had been waiting and waiting for Sister's voice. I had intended to call back, "Fabulous, I'm on my way," leap instantly to my feet, and get on with it. But I just sat, shaking all over, suddenly aware of my heart thumping, my pulse rate going up, and feeling hot and cold.

"Come on, Sheila," I heard Sister say again cheerfully, "we're ready." Somewhere behind me Muriel said, "Go on Sheila, we're all with you." I was thinking, *This is what I've been waiting for. This should be the beginning of the great moment, at last. . . . Or perhaps it won't be after all. . . .* I was terrified.

But I got to my feet, and then walked slowly and haltingly. I could hardly make it at all. Eventually I got into the treatment room, and hands guided me to the chair. I felt my way around it. In all the confusion of my mind I remember thinking that it was an odd sort of chair for a hospital—more like an office chair. It had arms that felt leathery and a headrest. I sat in it, gripping the arms as if my very life depended on hanging on. I could feel the nurses unwinding the bandages, and suddenly I did not want them to do it. Yet, at the same time, I couldn't do anything to stop them. I wanted to shout, "Don't. Please don't do it." Now that it had come, I just did not want to face the moment.

Then the bandages were off, and I still did not know the result, because I had my eyes shut tight. I heard Sister saying, "Come on, Sheila, open your eyes. The bandages are off . . ." I gripped the armrests even harder and opened my eyes.

What happened then was that I was suddenly hit—physically struck—by brilliance, like an immense electric shock into my brain and through my entire body. This utterly unimaginable, incandescent brightness flooded my being like a shock wave. There was white in front of me, a dazzling white that I could hardly bear to take in, a vivid blue that I had never thought possible. It was fantastic, mar-

velous, incredible. It was like the beginning of the
world.

I turned and looked the other way, and there were
greens, lots and lots of different greens, different
shades, all quite unbelievable, and at the same time
there flooded in sound, the sound of voices asking,
"Can you see, can you see?" But I was just so over-
whelmed and spellbound by the sensation that had
seized every inch of me—as if the sun itself had burst
into my brain and body and scattered every molten
particle of its light and color—that it took me some
time to say anything. I looked back at the blue and
said, "Oh it's blue, it's so beautiful."

"It's me," said Sister, walking towards me. The
blue I could see was her uniform, and she came
right up to me and touched me, saying, "Sheila, can
you see it?" But I was still not coherent, and I
turned away and exclaimed, "Green, it's wonderful."
This was Annette and Linda and Ann, who had
gathered around me. "It's us, it's our uniforms," they
said.

Then they realized I could see properly, because
there was something to my left that appeared to me
a sort of yellow color. I did not know what it was,
and asked, "What's that over there, that yellow
thing?" And they said, "It's a lamp, and it's really
cream color, pale cream." But they knew for certain
I could see it, though I had not known it was a lamp
and I had got the color wrong. My memory of colors
was pretty murky, but I could still identify the
strongest ones. Yet until that moment in my life I
had no idea that there could possibly exist so many
clear, clean colors.

All this, I know, took only a few seconds. Everything crowded in. Then, just as quickly, everything
started to go misty and blurred. The colors began to
fade and merge into one another, and I thought, *No,*

oh no, it's going. That's all there's going to be, I can't bear it . . . I was struck by a sudden terror and instinctively put my hand up to my eyes—and found there were tears streaming down my face. I thought, *Oh, thank goodness, it's not going, it's just the tears.* And I wept uncontrollably and could not stop, because of the joy and the shock that I still could not fully take in. At the same time, everyone around me—Sister, nurses and all sorts of people I did not know—were shaking my hand, and I could see just enough to realize that they, too, were crying and could not say anything for tears.

The memory of those few seconds is indelible: the wonder, the sense of disbelief yet belief, the sudden engulfing knowledge that I could see. *I could see!*

Then I had to have the bandages put back on again, but I did not care. I knew there was a flood of light outside, even if I had to be returned to the dark world from which I had come. And when the bandages were back on, I understood that I had never really known the depth of that former permanent darkness, because the recollection of the first brief sight of brilliance remained in my mind. The colors danced and merged still, coming and going in unending patterns, as in a child's kaleidoscope, exploding like fireworks. And as they did I said to myself, *It's still so beautiful,* and I knew I had escaped from the infinite black pit.

When I returned to the ward I was even shakier than when I had left for the treatment room. I wanted to shout out at everyone there, "I can see, I can see!" But what I managed was barely above a whisper. Everyone in the ward knew anyway. The news had gone before me, and I could feel how pleased everybody was for me, how overjoyed and overcome that it had happened. And this—the feeling that other people cared—was wonderful, too.

As I sat in an armchair in the ward, the thought was drumming away, *I must call Don, I must tell him*. Then I heard Jasmine. She had guessed I would want to phone immediately, and because I was still crying, she said, "Can I dial the number for you?" She had had the mobile telephone plugged in, and she asked, "Can I stand here while you tell him you can see?" I could feel her joy like a physical thing and hear it in her voice.

But, however perfect you imagine things might be, they never are, and when I dialed the number myself there was no answer at Don's clinic. He was out on his visits. I heard the phone ringing and ringing, and thought, *Don, answer, I've got to tell you, you must answer*. But the ringing tone went on and on until I put the receiver down. Then I tried the number of his radio-telephone service, so they could try his call sign, 269, and give him a message. It would not be the same as telling him myself, but he would get to know as soon as possible.

I got through to this number immediately. "I'd like you to give a message to 269."

"Yes, certainly. What's the message?"

"Just tell him I can see."

There was a pause, and the voice that came back sounded puzzled. "Oh. Tell him that you can see?"

"Yes. Just tell him that."

I put the phone down, feeling a bit deflated, because I really wanted to rush out of the hospital and wave all the traffic down on the road and tell them, or go and shout from the top of Everest, or go on the radio worldwide and say, over and over, "I can see, it's me, I can see!"

Instead, I phoned my brother, and all I kept saying was, "I can see, the colors are fabulous, and I never knew the world was so brilliant," and then I called my parents and Anita and practically everyone else I could think of. I gave them all the same message. No one at the other end had much of a chance to say anything back, but I knew everyone was thrilled for me. I spent a fortune in calls.

It was not until nearly midday that I heard from Don. He had received my message. He told me that he had been to see a patient and had got back to the car where Emma was sitting in the passenger seat waiting for him, when the call light of his radio telephone came on. He was nervous about answering, because he had been waiting all morning for a message; he sat there for a minute not daring to brace himself for the news, whether it would be infinitely good or heartbreakingly bad. He told me when he did pick up the telephone and the message came through, he just had no reply. He sat in the driving seat unable to grasp the sheer wonder of it all, and finally he put his arms around Emma, and said, "Emma, you'll never have to work again."

Later, when he came to see me that evening, we did not speak much at first. Neither of us could appreciate fully what had happened. We were so close, Don and I, that it was some time before we needed to put into words all the possibilities that were expanding in our minds, like a world suddenly starting to form, whirling around, taking shape and getting bigger and bigger all the time. Eventually all his sentences started with, "When you come home . . ." And each time there was something new he wanted to show me. We sat and talked and planned in the ward. He told me that the leaves were turning from green to red, and it meant something to me for the first time. He had built a new stone fireplace and could not wait for me to see it. We would go on vacation . . . Life began to unfold in front of me, and now—instead of being bound by the limits of my pool of blackness—it stretched on and out, full of light.

When Don had phoned at midday, the nurses had been bringing me my lunch. But I was too excited to eat. I kept thinking, *If those colors were so beautiful, what about the rest, what about everything else? What is it like outside?* I wanted to tear the bandages off and rush to the window and see everything.

I also wanted Dr. Shearing to come see me. He *had* worked a miracle, and I wanted him to share all my feelings and know what I thought about him and everything else. I kept asking Sister, "When will Dr. Shearing be coming?" I knew he had not been able to be in the treatment room that morning because he had been operating. "Oh, he'll be in as soon as he can," she would reply. "He's still in the operating room." I sat there for most of that Monday afternoon, thinking, *I do wish he would hurry up; I can't wait to tell him how fantastic it all is,* and I kept wondering if he knew that the operation had worked beyond our wildest dreams.

Then, at about four o'clock, I suddenly detected a familiar smell in the distance. It was the aroma of cigar smoke. Dr. Shearing! He was probably with Sister, discussing what had happened. Sure enough, I soon heard his footsteps approaching along the ward, and I sat up. When the footsteps stopped and I heard the voice say, "Hello, lassie, how are you?" all my words suddenly tumbled out and rushed away with me in a great surge of emotion. "Oh, it's so wonderful, it's fabulous, oh, I can't tell you, it's marvelous . . ." But his only comment was, "Yes, isn't it wonderful Notts Forest won on Saturday?"

I was flabbergasted. I could hardly believe my ears. I said, "Notts Forest? I don't care about football! I can *see*, that's the marvelous thing." He patted me awkwardly on the shoulder and left. A minute or two later, Muriel came up and said, "I wish you could have seen his face. It looked as if it had been lit up. He just stood there, smiling at you." And I realized that he had been at a loss for words. Gentle and humane person that he is, Dr. Shearing had used all the business about Nottingham Forest to sidestep something he was too moved to express.

I was able to appreciate a little of his reaction, but it was not until I went back to the hospital a year later that I learned the full story of how Dr. Shearing had really felt. At the hospital one of the patients recognized me, and, by chance, her father had been in at the same time as I had originally, but in the men's ward upstairs. She told me, "After Dr. Shearing had been to see you, he went up to the men's ward and went around telling everybody you could see, and how wonderful you thought it was, and how it really made him think that everything was worthwhile."

I then remembered talking to him when he was telling me about the failures he had had in operations, and how terrible and sad it was, that he had proved unable to do anything for these patients. I remember saying, "But the successes must be worth everything." He had agreed they were, and now I felt how tremendous it was that he had gone up to that ward and told everyone about it. He must have—or I certainly hope he must have—felt the immense joy of giving so much.

After Dr. Shearing had gone, I waited for visiting time, and I was inundated with visitors. Other than Don, who had come every day, and my mother and father and Graham, none of my friends had been in up to then. But that evening about ten people crowded around my bed. To every one of them I went on and on about what had happened during those two minutes in the treatment room. They just

about got hello and good-bye in and handed me
their presents of chocolates and flowers.

During the rest of my stay in the hospital, the
bandages were taken off each morning for a couple of
minutes, drops were put in my eyes, and clean bandages were put back. Apart from those few lucid, incandescent minutes, I inhabited my old world. But
increasingly it became less like that familiar, enclosed world as I began to know more and more of
what lay beyond. And yet every morning, when the
moment arrived for me to go to the treatment room,
I had a flicker of doubt. I always wondered, *Will it
be as bright again, will it be as beautiful?* Each morning it was, and the anxieties faded from my mind.

I enjoyed choosing things to look at during my
brief intervals of sight. One day I brought some of
the flowers from the ward with me to the treatment
room. When the bandages were removed and I had
recovered from the renewed shock of brilliance, I
looked down at the dahlias and saw that they were a
gorgeous yellow that I had never imagined, and that
they were intricately made. I felt guilty that I hadn't
liked them before, because they felt spiky and had
no scent. Another time I decided to look at my
bathrobe. This might sound trivial, but it was important to me to know what I was wearing and how
I appeared.

As I was looking down at my robe, I caught sight
of my hands and had a tremendous shock. I thought
they looked awful and could not keep my eyes off
them. "Annette, look at my hands. Aren't they terrible?" I called to one of the nurses.

She came over, looked at them quite closely and
asked, "What's terrible about them?"

"Well, look at them, look at the veins, and the
knuckles. The bones stick out. Don't they look
dreadful?"

"But they're perfectly normal."

"They can't be."

"But they are. Look at mine. Your hands are like everybody else's."

So I looked at her hands, and saw the veins standing out, and said, "Gosh, aren't they horrible things?" I always pictured them as smooth and nice. I was really quite upset, and disillusioned. When Don came in that evening, I said to him, "Look at my hands."

"Yes. Well, they're all right. What's the matter?"

"But they're horrible."

"No, they're not. They're beautiful hands."

"But look at the veins sticking out, and the knuckles. They're ugly."

"No, they're not. Wait till you've seen mine. You'll see the veins and everything. Everybody's hands are like that."

I really could not accept that. I went around for the next day or so tucking my hands out of sight in my dressing gown sleeves.

The following day Dr. Shearing came to examine me again. He said if I wanted I could go home the following day. I felt as a prisoner must when pardoned for a crime he never committed. I was so excited that I phoned Don immediately.

That night was another sleepless one, waiting for Friday, the day when I would see the outside world for the first time and really start my new life.

14

AT FIRST SIGHT

Don was due to pick me up at noon. All week he had been joking about having his hair dyed from gray to a different color. He said, "It's all right for you, you know. I've seen you. I knew what you looked like to start with. But you've never seen me. You could be in for a shock." My response was, "Whatever you look like, it won't make any difference." It had not occurred to me that from now on I would look at people, and what I saw would help to form my judgment of them—accurately or inaccurately—like the rest of the sighted world I was joining.

I waited, wearing dark glasses I had been given that morning. My eyes were still not accustomed to the general brilliance, and so they had to be shaded for the time being. I walked up and down the ward, still thrilled by the colors, dimmed as they were by my glasses. Even the very whiteness of the sheets and pillowcases on the beds impressed me. I looked at the bowls of flowers and thought to myself, "I don't believe in evolution. Those flowers were always like that, perfect in every detail, but waiting for me to see them, especially made for me." It was irrational, but that was the way I felt.

I sat by my bed, my cases packed, wondering what Don looked like, trying to imagine his face from the ideas I had received over the years. But it was no good. Then I heard the ward door open and Don coming down the ward. I thought, *Oh God, this is him. This is the moment,* and I looked up. I saw a stranger coming towards me and did not for an instant connect him with Don. I thought fleetingly, *Brown, suntanned, handsome,* and then, *It's Don!* He was so much more distinguished-looking and so very much more handsome than I could possibly have imagined. I was struck with the idea of how lucky I was to have a husband whom I not only loved for everything I had not been able to see, but with whom I instantly fell in love all over again for his appearance.

He came up to me and said, smiling, "Hello, Petal." My face told him, I am sure, all he needed to know about my reactions to his looks. I was grinning from ear to ear as I said, "Hello."

He picked up my cases and said, "Well, come on then, come and have a look at the outside world. Emma's waiting in the car." And I thought, *Emma, dear Emma, I shall be seeing her for the first time as well. What a day!* I could not get out of the ward fast enough, with everyone waving and wishing me good luck. Don and I went arm in arm through the doors, and I said good-bye to Sister and the other nurses. Then, when we reached the outer doors, it was like that first electric shock all over again.

The sunshine burst in on me, and once more I felt the entire Creation was being laid out for my personal benefit. At the same time I felt I was seeing for the first time something everyone else was used to and took for granted.

Beyond the sunshine and immediate glaring radiance, I saw a great expanse of green.

"What's that?" I asked Don.

"Why, it's grass, of course."

Grass? Of course. It had to be. I had felt it

through the soles of my shoes. "But it's so green. I can't believe it. Is it always like this?"

Don said it was, but I had to kneel down and touch it to make sure it was what I had felt before.

"But it's all different shades, all different greens. Look at those patches. Even the separate blades seem to differ in color."

"Yes. It's always like that."

We walked over towards the car, and Don went ahead to let Emma out. The next thing I knew, she came bounding out of the car, and I could see the sun shining and glinting on her coat as she bounced up to me. I put my arms around her and saw her tail going, making her whole body move. I cried, "Oh, Don, isn't she *beautiful*." People had told me she was chocolate brown, and that was the main impression I'd had of her appearance. I had also been told that she had a white patch on her chest, and her nose and eyes were brown, but none of it had really meant much to me. But now I could *see* her! No one had ever described her properly.

Her ears were a gingery color. As the sun shone on them they turned to a pale ginger. Her lovely brown nose glistened. There was a gingery part along her nose towards her eyes, and the auburn along her back was rich and deep; it shaded off down her legs and along her flanks into a soft brown. She was more gorgeous than I could ever have imagined in a thousand years. I said, "Oh, Emma, you're so beautiful! Nobody ever told me. Everybody said you were brown, but nobody told me you were a hundred shades of brown!" Her reply was to wag her tail even more vigorously, take one of the smaller bags from me and go rushing around with it on the grass. We had not been together for ten days, and she was as happy to meet me as I was to see her for the first time. She went off towards the car holding the bag and dove into the back seat with it to make sure I was not going to leave her again. If she had the bag, it stood to reason that I would have to stay with her!

I got in, and Emma kept touching me with her nose while I stroked her head. It was odd to sit in the car that I had been in so many times but had never seen. It was odd, too, to watch Don driving, changing gear and steering. I had never thought about it and had barely appreciated that so much was involved. I kept looking at him and thinking, *Isn't he good-looking? Isn't he fabulous? Aren't I lucky?* He looked at me too from time to time, not saying much at all.

Once out of the hospital gates I began to stare out of the windows, and all sorts of things came tumbling in on my consciousness. "Those orange lines down there, what are they for?"

"Oh, they're double yellow lines. There are single yellow lines as well. They tell you where you can park and where you can't."

"When did they put them there?"

"They've been there for years."

"Are you sure?"

"Mm, . . . They've been there for ages."

It was slightly unnerving seeing things I had never known existed. "Don, look. There are all sorts of white lines along the road."

"Yes. They've been there even longer."

I thought that no one would ever have dreamed of telling me there were white and yellow lines on the roads; they wouldn't have thought I'd be interested. Seeing them, I was fascinated. The fields, too, were incredible to me. I had no idea they were all so grassy, or that there were so many trees.

"Don, look at the trees. Are there always as many as this?"

"Yes. They're all over the place, thousands of them. Even in the city."

Of course I knew there were trees. I'd always been aware of them, and could hear them rustling when the wind blew. But I had never imagined that they were everywhere, and I could not get over the different shapes—some round, some tall, and all in varying, breathtaking shades of green.

Don said, "All trees are like that. Even the same kind of tree—oak, beech, chestnut, or whatever—can vary in shape when you look at it." And I looked at them as we drove along, with the sun catching them and somehow becoming entangled in the branches and leaves and throwing moving shadows, so that the trees looked as if they were made in layers, like frills.

I could see the leaves being moved by the wind and said, "They look as if they're doing a dance in the wind."

All the people intrigued me, and I am sure that Don, kind as he is, must have wanted to laugh at me. "Gosh," I said, "look at all the people on the pavement. They've all got different colored clothes. It's fantastic."

But Don did not laugh. He just said, "Yes, when you were in the car before, you didn't realize they were there, because you couldn't hear them once you were on the move." He was right. I had known there were countless people all around, but when you can't see, a car insulates you; you don't think about all the human beings outside it doing their shopping, going to work or standing talking.

I kept saying to Don, "Look at the houses, they're all different, they've all got different colored doors." Yellow lines, white lines, posters, buses, road signs, shops . . . it was like a journey to a place I had never been before, someplace I had never thought existed, a new world, all rotating past the car window like an enormous merry-go-round.

When we were almost home I remembered my flowers. I had so many beautiful bouquets and bunches of roses, dahlias and freesias that even the hospital had more than enough for other patients, and had said they did not mind my taking some home. But in the excitement I had forgotten all about them. I was rather upset at the thought of offending the people who had sent or brought them. "Can't we go back?" I asked Don, but he said, "Oh, it's a terribly long way, and we're nearly home now. It doesn't matter." But it did matter.

Another thought soon pushed this one aside. My Siamese cats had been boarded out. My friend Pat, whom I had met because she herself bred Siamese, had taken Ming and a four-week-old kitten, and other people had kindly agreed to take the rest of my brood. I was dying to see them all, now that I knew that colors were nothing like I had imagined. "Oh Don," I said, "are the cats all right? Can we bring them home this afternoon?" But he just said, "Now, don't worry about the cats. Everything's sorted out. You just come home, and everything will be fine."

By this time we were on the road where we lived. It all looked lovelier than I'd imagined, with trees and roses in people's front gardens. Then we drove up to the gate. I got out, and Emma leaped over the seat, and got in front of me, tail wagging. As we opened the door, she rushed in first, and went straight to fetch me various gifts to show how pleased she was that I was home.

I walked into the living room, *my* living room, and saw it for the first time. Like everything else, it was different from my mental images. Because so

much had been dark and dismal in my mind, I
hadn't pictured what a charming room it was. I suddenly thought that Don had had the rich red carpet
put down especially for me, but when I kneeled
down and touched it, I realized he hadn't. It was the
same carpet we had always had.

"What do you think of the fireplace?" Don asked
anxiously. It was great-looking—all the stone he had
carefully laid, with fawns and pinks. I noticed the
horse brasses that I had cleaned every week and saw
their sparkle for the first time.

Then I suddenly caught sight of the biggest bou-
quet of flowers imaginable in the middle of the
room—pinks, roses, dahlias, all overflowing the bowl
and dominating the room. "Don," I said, "you
shouldn't have. They're wonderful. What a home-
coming! No wonder you didn't mind about the hospital flowers!"

So much for my anxiety in the car. In the next instant, my other small worry was dispelled. I realized,
turning away from the flowers, and with quite a
start, that there was someone else in the room. I
caught a movement in the corner of my eye, looked
around, and saw a woman standing over by the window. I had no idea who it was.

"Who's that?" I asked, staring at her. (Whose face
could I have recognized immediately?) She started to
laugh but would not say anything, and I racked my
brains trying to figure out who it was. Then she said,
still laughing, "It's me." Instantly I knew the voice.
"Pat," I said, "what are you doing here?"

"I've brought your cats."

"You mean Ming and the kitten. How nice of
you!"

"No, not just Ming and the kitten. I've got the rest
as well. I thought you'd want to see them all as soon
as you could."

Pat disappeared into the kitchen, and a second later, Ming came through the door. What struck me immediately was how intensely blue her eyes were, and as I took in her other details—her shining black face, her paws, her ears—I reacted in the same way as when I had seen Emma for the first time. With Ming, and with my other cats as they came in later, I was not at all prepared for the variety of colors and shades that no one and no textbook had ever told me about. I had originally chosen to have Siamese because they were so smooth and svelte, but to see them was a revelation, and the greatest pleasure of all was to watch them move. It was as if they floated over the ground.

Eventually Don had to go back to the clinic, and Pat had to go, too. This left me in the house on my own (apart from the animals), and I liked the idea, because it gave me an opportunity to look at everything I wanted to see. I sat on the sofa, with Emma next to me, and I looked at her. Don had often said that Emma had an old-fashioned look, and I saw the expression he meant when we were together again that afternoon: a look that suggested great moral virtue. I smiled at her, putting out my hand to stroke her. She moved her head forward towards my hand, and I thought, *I wonder if she's been doing that for the past ten years when I put out my hand without knowing where she was?*

I loved to sit and look at Emma and watch her face change to a kind of delight, with her ears going up, and the end of her tail brushing the carpet. As we sat there, I thought of all the things I wanted to do, now that I was home.

One of the first items on my list was to look into a mirror. I had seen Don, Emma, Ming and the other cats. But I had not yet seen myself! I was more than a little apprehensive, for I had no idea what to expect. One half of my mind prompted, *Come on, get it over with. It's got to be done, and waiting won't alter the result for better or worse.* The other half of my mind insisted on delaying. I suppose I sat on the couch for nearly a quarter of an hour, stroking Emma, summoning up the will to go and do what had to be done.

When I was blind I had never really thought much about the existence of mirrors, and the house, naturally, was not overendowed with them. I supposed there was one in the bathroom for Don to see himself shaving. When I was sitting there, turning these thoughts over in my mind, I looked around the room again. In addition to mirrors, I had never thought very much about the existence of pictures on the wall either.

Don used to paint in his spare time, and he had hung some of his canvases. One that he had done was a copy of Rembrandt's *Man in the Golden Helmet.* I was fascinated by the gold and the intricate work on the helmet. To the left, I recalled, there was a seascape. When I went to look at this, I encountered for the first time the difficulty which was to arise quite frequently in those first few days out of the hospital. This was the problem of relating the reality of the image that was transmitted through the eyes to the brain, to a previous reality conditioned by touch or verbal description. I could immediately identify some objects I saw for the first time, although I still do not know why. But with others I had not the least notion of what they might be until I felt them. I could make no sense of the seascape whatsoever. When Don brought me a cup of tea the following morning, I looked at the cup and had no idea what it was until I touched it.

At last, after examining our various pictures, I
went into the bathroom and there confronted myself.
I saw—as with Don coming up the ward, but even
more unnervingly—a total stranger. I did not know
what to think. The lips moved when I moved mine,
and the eyes blinked when I blinked. I suppose I
should not have expected sudden recognition. How
could I suddenly form an opinion of myself? Of my
hair I thought, *Not bad, not bad, it's really just
about the same color as Emma's.*

The feature I kept on looking at was my nose. I
put my hand up to touch it, because I couldn't believe it was mine. It felt as it always had; my nose
hadn't grown. But I was appalled by its grotesque
and clown-like appearance. It dominated my entire
face! Why had no one told me? Don, my mother and
all my friends must have known about it all along
and kept quiet out of politeness. I was so upset, I
could not look any longer. I felt miserable that I had
a nose that stuck out so far, and it took me a long
time before I was reassured that it was not extraordinary.

To get away from the thought of my nose I went
into the bedroom and looked in the closet at all the
clothes that friends had helped me buy, or that I had
bought myself after having them described to me by
a salesman. Some were awful. There were colors that
did not go with one another, and others that were
far too bright and gaudy for my taste. I was quite
taken with some dresses I hadn't previously liked.
The texture of the material had not pleased me, and
I was surprised to find they were very pretty. Now
the exciting thing was the prospect of being able to
go out and choose my own clothes and start a fresh
wardrobe. That cheered me up, big nose or not.

I went back into the living room and sat down,
looking around me once more. I adored the curtains,

the carpet and the wallpaper. Everything was so colorful and looked to me fresh and new. I had lived here for years, but it was like being in a different home. It was not the home of my imagination at all but a brighter, more spacious, more comfortable place altogether.

By this time I was getting hungry, particularly since I had not had anything at lunchtime. I realized I would have to go out to the stores to buy something. I was itching to do this, in fact—to go out on my own. What would it be like? The stores were not far away, on the corner, and I knew them well. I wanted to see them. I found my shopping bag in the hall and walked to the front door, Emma sensing we were about to go on an outing and getting excited. But at the door I stopped. Exactly how would I do it? I felt apprehensive. My original idea had been that I would go with Emma on the lead. But now I decided that for this first time I had better put on her harness and let her take me along. Then, when I was thoroughly used to going out, we could dispense with the harness.

When I picked the harness off the peg, Emma bounced up and down, barked and shook herself. She was overjoyed that after all this time of separation we were at last going out together again. It would be like old times for her, though not for me. I asked Emma to find the shops, and she took me out of the gate and along the sidewalk. But as soon as we were on our way, I saw the pavement rushing by under me. It was so unexpected and frightening that I had to tell Emma to stop. In a moment I recovered and we went on again. But then I saw the fence coming at us at a headlong rate and the trees seeming to fly towards us as if they were going to knock us down. Looking down again, I saw that the pavement and even the shadows of the lamp posts were sweeping along towards me like solid black bars, making me think I would trip. It was no good. Once more I had to tell Emma to stop. Logically, I knew I was moving, and not the lamp posts, the pavement or the shadows. But as far as I was concerned visually, the reverse was happening.

I decided to give it another try, but the same thing happened again. I was panic-stricken. I had to keep stopping to reassure myself that it really was me in motion, and each time we stopped Emma sat down and looked at me with those great brown eyes full of questions. She wanted to know what was happening—why, after ten years together, I was behaving in this peculiar fashion. In the end the only solution I could think of was to close my eyes and let Emma carry on as usual. And this is how we finally arrived at the shops.

I opened my eyes, and we were outside the produce market. Immediately I was hit by a mass of color, and that, mixed with some relief at actually being there, made me think that the trip there was worth it after all. I was astonished at the sight of all the fruit and vegetables and flowers in the window and saw to my immense surprise that each apple was different in its redness or greenness, and that no two potatoes or heads of lettuce looked alike. How could there be so many shades and varieties of color?

Apart from this, there were a lot of things in the window that I could not identify at all. Once again I was coming up against the problem of not being able to relate my previous tactile impressions to my present vision. Perhaps I had already given my brain enough to cope with that day. Seeing was miraculous, but, in a way, I had to learn to see as well.

The grocer knew me and was delighted at the success of my operation, and didn't mind my touching things I could not recognize. There was something on the counter that, try as I would, I could not put a name to. I could see some red and green and a shape, but the object would not fit any description I could think of. Then I touched it. I realized I was seeing leaves and flowers. It was a plant, a poinsettia. I could not understand why I had not immediately known what it was. Then I pointed to something on the shelf, and asked, "What's that?" "Celery." "And those?" "Beets," the grocer said. So I went on and finished up buying tomatoes because they had the most gorgeous color of all.

On our way back, I determined to keep my eyes open, which led to an odd incident. I was again in a state of nerves, when I saw a young boy coming toward us. As usual, I was talking to Emma as we walked, and I said, "Now there's someone coming, Emma, do be careful." As I said it, I thought, *Now I must take action. I must get around this boy. But how? How do I do it?* It did not occur to me that I was abandoning my trust and faith in Emma. I thought, *I'll step aside to the right, and we'll avoid him that way.* So, when he was nearly up to us, I stepped to the side of the pavement to go right. In the very same second, Emma had decided the best way to take us past the boy was to go left. I released the harness, and we landed on the ground in a heap, while the boy went merrily on, unaware of our predicament. I felt dreadful, and I knew by Emma's expression she could not figure out what had happened. She yawned, not out of boredom, but rather embarrassment.

She sat looking at me with an anxious, quizzical expression which said, "Why ever did you do that? In ten years you've never done that before. What's happened?" I said, "Oh, Emma, I'm sorry. I shouldn't have put your harness on." I decided that I had been expecting too much of her. I had virtually been asking her to stand by me until I had the courage to go out on my own. It was not fair. From then on, whenever we went out, I would simply have to put her on a lead and learn how to manage myself.

We somehow got home from the store, and then I took great delight in being able to empty my shopping bag and see what I was going to use to prepare a meal. But one thing I was already beginning to realize was that it took a great deal of concentration to look at objects. The mental effort involved in seeing was something I had not suspected would be required. I had imagined that once I got my sight back I would be able to see, and that would be that. But it was not the case. It was like suddenly being given an extra limb and having to work hard at getting used to putting it to the best advantage. But it was exciting, too.

When I looked into the food cupboard for the first time, I found an Aladdin's cave full of cans and packets and jars which I did not know by sight, but which I had used before. They had taken on a new existence. I came across a packet that was red, yellow and white, and I thought, *What's this?* It said SALT on it, but I saw the word merely as an arrangement of different-shaped letters. Although years before I had been able to read print, I needed time to regain this faculty. I could remember some printed words in my mind and was able to write them down when I could not see. But, the other way around—being presented with words via my eyes and required by the brain to attach a meaning to them—was something far more difficult.

So, to begin with, I identified the salt by the old method, taste, and I related this to the color of the box. Cereal packets were yellow or white with a pattern on them; baked bean cans were a distinctive turquoise blue; and so on.

I enjoyed going through the food cupboard on that first afternoon, and I enjoyed even more the preparation of the meal, with all the reds and greens of the salad dazzling me, even down to the simple business of running water from the tap over the lettuce. The way the water glistened and swirled, caught the light, and made a waterfall pattern in the sink fascinated me. Once I had set the table and was waiting for Don to come home, I went out into the garden, my lovely garden. I was so proud of it as I walked about, with Emma running along beside me.

When I was blind, there had been times when I hated the trees in that garden. The branches were always getting tangled in my hair, and if I did take a walk around the lawn, I used to have to keep in mind the presence and arrangement of the three apple trees to make sure I did not collide with them. The apple trees, in fact, had been nothing more than rather ogrelike obstacles, to be avoided and shunned. Now they not only looked incapable of harm, but beautiful, too. And at the edge of the grass was our willow tree. I could not get over its sheer grace. The leaves were green on one side and silver on the other. For a moment I thought my eyes really had got it wrong. No one had ever told me that trees could have silver leaves. It was while I was looking at the willow that I noticed the sky for the first time—how the clouds moved, sailing along, with great billows of white on blue. I heard the car drive up and the gate latch click. Don was back.

Joining me on the lawn, he said, "Hello. How have you been getting on? What have you been doing?"

"Oh, looking at everything, you know."

"What are you looking at now?"

"Well, to tell you the truth, I'm waiting to see the sunset."

Don had often described the sunset to me and no one could have done it better or more vividly. But as I stood with him in the garden watching the sun going down and the colors beginning to change in fractions of a second, I knew that there was no substitute for sight. Until that day all I had ever had were secondhand sunsets.

On this evening we stood and watched together. The sun disappeared, and the clouds and sky around were streaked with gold and purple. It was perfect, and to end my first full day of sight nothing could have equaled it.

15

A NEW LIFE

For the first few seconds after I woke up the following morning, everything seemed normal. It was no different from any other morning, from the ten thousand other times I had awakened. In front of me was a blank, grayish mist. Then I remembered. I could see! I had only to open my eyes, and I could see! It was the first morning of a new life. But, in my drowsiness, I wondered, *Is it all really true? Dare I open my eyes?*

The night before, tired as I was, I had not wanted to go to sleep. It had seemed such a waste to spend eight hours with my eyes shut. I had lain there feeling happier than I had ever been in my life. Emma had got into her basket at the foot of the bed, and I had looked at the wallpaper, unable to keep my eyes off it. It was so pretty, with cascades of blossoms on a deep rose background. Don was in bed beside me, and I remember him saying, "We can go anywhere we want, you know." I really did think that the world, at last, was mine. I was still looking at the wallpaper when we put the light out.

Now I opened my eyes. Immediately I saw that the wallpaper was still there. I could read, I could take Emma for walks, I could see everything I had heard about and been told about and never properly known. An astonomer who sees a new planet must, I thought, feel like this, or an explorer who comes to the edge of a plateau and finds below him miles and miles of unexplored territory. As I lay daydreaming, I saw the sun streaming through the curtains and Emma lying curled up in her basket.

Then Don stirred and said he would get up and make some tea. Emma woke too and got out of her basket. She stretched sleepily right down on her forelegs with eyes half-closed against the brightness of the day, but looked up at me, full of affection. She gave her usual brisk and vigorous good-morning shake and then, wagging her tail, jumped up on the bed. I had heard all this every day but never before had seen what happened.

When Don came in with the tea I said to him, "I wonder how long it will be before she realizes I can see?" Emma had obviously not yet grasped the fact, and I wondered whether it would dawn on her gradually or suddenly. Then something odd happened. As I was watching Don pour the tea and start to get dressed, I really noticed his legs for the first time and said, "Don, your legs."

"What about my legs?"

"Aren't they strange?" I started to giggle because they looked so peculiar to me.

Poor Don was a bit upset. He looked down and,

with a great muster of dignity said, "They're perfectly normal legs."

"But they can't be."

"Yes, they are."

"But they're all wrong somehow. They don't seem to fit the rest of your body."

He then turned around and hurriedly put on his trousers to cover his legs and hide them from my critical gaze. When I got out of bed a second or two later, I stopped laughing. I saw that my legs looked peculiar as well, amazingly disproportionate.

Soon I discovered something else. We were eating breakfast, and I put my fork towards a piece of bacon. Somehow the two did not connect. I could see the bacon, and I could see the prongs of the fork near it, but I could not bring the two together. The coordination was beyond me and—although it was an admission of a temporary setback, even an unforeseen defeat—I had to feel for my food with my knife and fork. I stopped concentrating on looking and went back to touch, but at least I had the pleasure of seeing my food, since sight does add to the appetite.

Over coffee, Don said, "Where would you like to go today?" He had arranged to have a week off from the clinic and was longing to take me on all sorts of trips in the car. Before he asked I knew where I wanted to go first—Newstead Abbey, which was only a twenty-minute drive from Nottingham. Once it was the home of Lord Byron, and I had been there many times when I was blind. I could almost feel the atmosphere of the old abbey and would imagine Byron writing poetry under the trees or riding his horse along the paths. I used to go around and feel the trees, knowing there were great masses of rhododendrons, and I would listen to the waterfalls. I was dying to see it all.

Don agreed to take me there. When we arrived we

walked to a lake which stretched like a great mirror.
There were moorhens and swans floating on it, attached to their shimmering reflections. Eventually
we came to the waterfalls. The sun was shining, and
it caught the water, turning it into a cascade of dia-
monds that whirled and danced over the stones. The
colors were changing in a halo over the falls. I could
not take my eyes off it, and Don almost had to drag
me to look at the flowers he had seen: dahlias and
chrysanthemums in a blaze of yellows and bronzes
and scarlets. To me it was as if all the color in the
world had suddenly been amassed on that spot.
Then I caught sight of a stone wall, a part of the old
abbey, and went over to see it. It was mottled all
over with pinks, whites, yellow, gray and brown,
with mosses and lichen growing in the crevices, all
made up of a million tiny details.

There was one last thing I had to see, and that
was Byron's memorial to his Newfoundland dog,
Boatswain. We reached the little square stone edifice
at the top of some steps. Emma went all around it,
very interested. And Don read to me what Byron
had written about the dog. The words on the stone
said that Boatswain possessed "Beauty without Van-
ity, Courage without Ferocity, and all the Virtues of
Man without his Vices." I wished that I had written
that, but in praise of Emma.

Every day we went someplace different, and every
morning I went into the garden to look at things.
One time, as we were waiting to go out, I called to
Don, "Come and have a look at this bird."

"Yes," he said, puzzled, "what's the matter with
it?"

"There's nothing the matter with it, but look, it's
sitting there in the branches."

"Yes," he said patiently, "I can see."

He did not get the point of my excitement, but I

should not have expected him to. I had to explain. I had known, because I had either been told or read it, that birds sat in trees. I had always been aware of birds around me somewhere. I could even tell the difference between some birds by the sound of their chirping. But my mind had never been able to connect birds with trees. I could never put them together somehow. It sounds mad, but it was so. And here I was actually seeing a bird in a tree.

On the last morning of our vacation, Don had a brilliant idea. "What about going up to Yorkshire, to Flamborough Head?" I knew that it was supposed to be very beautiful, and I could not wait to get in the car and start. I was longing for my first view of the sea.

It was a long drive, almost a hundred miles, and on the way countryside rolled by. Sometimes we would be going past a church at the bottom of a hill, and at the next moment we were at the top, looking over undulating greenness. I remember learning about contours in geography, but I had never before seen what they really were.

Don drove the car up to the lighthouse at Flamborough Head, and we got out, with Emma running ahead. A second or so after hearing a great booming and roaring, I saw the sea. I could scarcely believe the endless movement—such brilliance, such force of motion. The sea seemed to gather strength, pause for a moment of silence, and then come roaring in, dashing and thundering against the foot of the cliffs, while in the circle formed by the coast, the water appeared to boil. The first time this happened, I grabbed Don's arm. I felt sure the cliff was trembling and would crumble under the assault. But when the wave retreated from the worn foot of the cliff, I realized that this had been happening for centuries, and that I was quite safe.

Emma loved Flamborough too. She ran about and helped us when we went down to the beach to collect some pebbles and shells. She dashed in and out of the sea, shaking herself with happiness. I picked up all sorts of different stones from the beach, and we took them as mementos. And, back home, I looked at Don's seascape again. It made sense to me at last.

But among the tumbling impressions of that week, there was a touch of sadness, too. I had time to go through all the drawers and cabinets, and I came across old letters, forgotten books and magazines, and photographs. It was looking at the photographs that brought home to me that there were some things I had not known about when I was blind and would almost have preferred to keep that way. I found a lot of photographs of Emma, all lovely, from the age of a few weeks, showing what a gorgeous, lively little puppy she must have been. Others showed her later, in the fullness of her vigor and looks, and still more continued up to the present. Looking at them one after the other, I could see the process of Emma's growing up and getting older. I knew she was nearly eleven, but I never thought of her as that old. Her age did not mean anything to me until I saw those photographs, and then it suddenly hit me, even though she still looked her lovely self, with not a gray hair. I was confronted all at once with the fact that, for a dog, Emma was getting on.

And sadness was not the only unpleasant sensation. During the week, I went one afternoon to do some shopping in Nottingham, and this made me realize that the possession of sight would not automatically make life easier. I got off the bus and went out of the bus station. To say I was shocked would be nowhere near the truth. I was, all at once, scared out of my wits. I was with Emma on the lead, and as we

emerged, I saw people, thousands of people, and cars
and buses and cyclists going past, all mingled in a
great melee. I could not believe there could be so
many people, and not one of them took any particular notice of Emma and me. Why should they have?
I was no longer blind, and Emma was not wearing a
guide-dog's harness. I had always relied on Emma
implicitly to take me through crowds and people,
but now I was bumped and jostled, and I was making no effort to get out of the way.

It was frightening, but we went on, and then I
happened to look up and see an enormously tall office building, part of the new center of Nottingham.
I had never thought anything could be so towering
or so threatening. It seemed to sway. I knew the
clouds were going past above, but it looked as if the
buildings were moving and not the sky. Feeling
dizzy, I finally managed to look away and get back to
the business of dividing everything into moving and
nonmoving obstacles, just as Emma had done for me
all those years. Emma, of course, trotted along, and
although she was still not used to being out with me
without her harness, she was very much like any
other dog on the lead.

But there came a moment when Emma sensed I
was in trouble, and she reverted immediately to the
role she knew best. We were going over a crossing
controlled by traffic lights. I waited for the green
light, and, just as important, listened for the bleep-
ing and the traffic stopping, because I still relied on
hearing a great deal. Halfway across the road I was
aware that there was something in our path. I had
no idea what it was. The image was there, but my
brain would not translate for me. I stood with
Emma in the middle of the crossing in front of this
object. Then Emma came to the rescue. From walking to heel, she came out in front of me and started

pulling left on the lead. I followed. She took me down the middle of the road, then across to the opposite pavement. When I turned and looked back at the crossing, I saw the bewildering object from a different angle and recognized what it was: one of those very long, flat trailers. It was empty and had stopped, straddled over the crossing.

On the bus that took me home I was able to look closely at the other passengers. People were a continuing source of amazement to me: some happy, others miserable-looking, some I thought I would like to know, but a lot more I would have run a mile from. All in all, I was disappointed by their appearances. If they had had a uniformity in my blind thoughts, at least they shared a certain imagined handsomeness, and I had never allowed for human beings' looking ugly, grotesque and even repulsive. In front of me sat a man whose neck bulged and rolled over his collar, and further down the bus was a bald man. Baldness, in particular, horrified me then, although by now I have become used to it.

Of course I was particularly startled at how different my family and friends looked from the way I had imagined them. When I answered the door one day and saw a man standing there, I had no idea until he spoke that it was my brother, Graham. And when my mother came over, I looked at her and said, "My goodness, haven't you gone gray? When did that happen?" I was tactless and possibly unkind in these encounters without meaning to be. It was only the surprise of reality that made me so.

I also took some time to get used to the idea of facial expressions. I looked at Don from time to time and thought, *People don't have one face, they have hundreds*. In a blind world there is only one hazy idea of what a face might be. There is no idea that the face is capable of change through laughter, sadness or any other expression. My own face, too, was changing. During that first week our friends Eddy and Mike Blain visited, and after they had been with us about half an hour, Mike said, "You've changed."

"Whatever do you mean?"

"Well, your face has changed."

"My face? How?"

"I don't really know. But it's different . . . I don't know, I suppose it looks somehow more alive, Sheila. You're using expression."

And it suddenly struck me that he must be right, and that the slight stiffness I had begun to feel in my face had nothing to do with the operation, as I had thought. Instead, it was caused by using facial muscles I had never used before. I suppose that children pick up expressions from their parents and from other children. But, never having seen a face well enough to mimic, I was now making up for lost time. I was glad Mike told me that my face had become alive.

Before the operation, when I went out with Don I would be with him, yet among a lot of people. But unless he was talking directly to me or I could hear him, I would feel that the circuit between us had somehow been switched off. After I could see, it was marvelous to be able to look across a room full of people and see him instantly, and, no matter how many people were around, smile and see him smile back.

The time came all too quickly for Don, after that wonderful week, to go back to the clinic. Eventually I, too, went back to work. Emma was a little more used to being on the lead, but it must have been strange for her going on the familiar morning journey into Nottingham without having to take charge.

She was still a bit puzzled and looked at me occasionally before we were going out as if she wanted to say, "Where's my harness? I don't understand." When we got to work, we went up to the door, and I thought, *I suppose this is the right place, but the door looks strange*. It was as if I had never known it. Yet as soon as I touched the handle, I knew I was right.

Inside, too, was like somewhere I had never known, utterly different from the idea I had built up. When I reached the switchboard I had worked at for so long, I could hardly believe my eyes. My braille machine was there still, ready for use. I hadn't thought of braille in the past few weeks. I felt as if I were an archeologist discovering a long-hidden relic from the past. Emma did not seem to mind, though. She went right to her basket and settled down.

At first I couldn't manage the new way. It was too hard to operate the switchboard visually. I learned in time, but at the beginning I reverted to working it as I had always done, by touch. Similarly, it was difficult to write messages instead of using the braille machine. At home I had started to teach myself to read again. It came slowly, but no matter how hard it was, nothing could diminish the sheer pleasure of being given back the ability to read, and I spent my time surrounded by books and magazines.

I went on working at the garage for some time, until, in fact, I decided to start writing this book. Gradually I learned to operate the switchboard by sight, and to write down all my messages. I was reminded of my former way of life quite dramatically and painfully when the question arose of training my replacement. This was to be my friend Kath, with her guide-dog Rachel bringing her to work. I had to show her how to use the switchboard, and seeing her work was like seeing myself as a ghost.

It was such a strange feeling. I could not believe that I had once been like that. But it came back to me in all sorts of ways. Kath felt my pen and pad and laughed. "They're no good to me," she said. I remembered how I used to feel—not wanting to admit that such things existed, things that I could not use. But even now, with my experience, I realized I still did not know how best to help Kath.

I kept wanting to tell her how to do something more quickly because I could see it. Someone would call, and instantly I could see what was happening and what number it was. But at the same time I could see Kath running her hand along the board, feeling for the movement of the indicator to answer the call. I was so frustrated by this that I wanted to say to her, "No, you're on the wrong side, it's over the other side, it's the one at the top." But I knew I would not be helping her if I did. It was heartrending, and nothing else since leaving the hospital has moved me so much. Suddenly I knew how people must have looked at me. It hurt particularly because Kath was such a capable blind person and such a good friend, and I could hardly bear it when I saw her feeling around her desk for her tea.

But life went on. Emma realized in time that I could see, and this happened, as I thought it might, as a result of one special incident. She was still in the habit Don had related to me of patiently waiting for the cats to finish their food every evening. Having perfected a method of stealing across the kitchen floor without my hearing her, she would go and polish off what was left. The first I would know about it was always the rattle of empty feeding bowls, when it was too late for anything to be done. One evening, however, I saw Ming come away from her supper, having left a little meat in the bowl as usual, and then I saw Emma, full of stealth, do a slow-motion walk towards the bowl. She was just about to put her great brown nose into it, when I shouted at her, "Emma, leave it!"

It was as if someone had fired a shotgun behind her. She spun around and looked at me with an expression I had never seen before: amazement, shock perhaps, even a hint that she had encountered the supernatural. "Yes," I said, "I can see. You were going to finish that off, weren't you?" She came over to me, pushed her nose into my hand and wagged her tail rather tentatively, as if she wished to say, "What's all this about? I don't understand this at all."

Yet I think she did understand. After that, when she went on the lead, she started to pull, bark at other dogs, and stop to sniff at trees—things that the correct, dignified, working Emma would never have dreamed of doing. But now she did not have to work, nor, because she was eleven, was there any question of her being anyone else's guide-dog. She had earned her freedom. When off the lead, she was a joy to watch, running along with her nose to the ground, stopping to investigate every blade of grass, her tail waving high in the air. And she seemed to share my joy in being able to see her.

But being able to enjoy Christmas to the full, more than anything else, summed up what sight meant to me. When I was a child I had always felt sad and frustrated at Christmas because I knew the town would be decorated with lights, trees and an enormous illuminated picture of Santa Claus. And in the shops there would be a host of things that my mother would describe, but that I could never enjoy through window shopping. I could put out a hand and touch them, of course, but it was not the same. However, I had always put up decorations at home.

I used to sit down, loving the idea that the house was properly decorated and that I had done it.

The Chistmas following my operation I bought more decorations than ever before and added them to the ones I already had. I also bought a huge tree, and I hung tinsel everywhere. Don came home with some lights for the tree, and when we switched them on, I felt that I was six again, only better. The pleasure I had from writing my own Christmas cards, and from being able to know as soon as I opened the envelope who had sent us cards, was indescribable. On Christmas Day itself I felt pure joy watching Don open each present. Whether it was a shirt or after-shave lotion, I had chosen it myself.

A year has gone by since then, a year in which I have gradually become more used to, more practiced in, what I can do with vision. But to this day, I have not lost my sense of wonder. When I hear people in the street complaining about the price of potatoes or coal going up again, I want to remind them just how lucky they are simply to be able to see the sky and the clouds.

Don and I think ourselves particularly lucky. On December 21, 1976, I had a baby daughter, Kerensa Emma Louise. (The middle name was chosen, of course, for a very good chocolate-brown reason.) We were blessed with a beautiful baby.

Yet when Kerensa was born, one prayer remained to be answered. Dr. Shearing had told us that she would have a fifty-fifty chance of perfect vision. And, much as my mother reasoned before I was born, we knew it was a chance that had to be taken. Dr. Shearing also warned us, however, that we would not know whether she could see until six weeks after her birth. "The eyes," he said, "don't focus properly till then."

The six weeks after Christmas went by, and we

grew more and more anxious. Don held out toys for
her, hoping for some sign that she could see. One
day he was bending over her cot, and, for some reason, he stuck his tongue out at her. She gurgled happily. Then she put *her* tongue out at *him*.

In amazement I cried, "She saw you do it! She can
see!" Don and I hugged one another and picked Kerensa out of her cot, and all three of us hugged again.
Then Emma came to see what the fuss was and
joined in, her tail wagging.

"She can see," we said again and again. All our
dreams had come true.